JUST
SPELLS

BHAVANA SHARMA

HEALTH HARMONY

An imprint of
B. Jain Publishers (P) Ltd.
An ISO 9001 : 2000 Certified Company
USA—EUROPE—INDIA

JUST SPELLS

First Edition: 2008
2nd Impression: 2010

Published by Kuldeep Jain for

HEALTH HARMONY

An imprint of
B. JAIN PUBLISHERS (P) LTD.
An ISO 9001 : 2000 Certified Company
1921/10, Chuna Mandi, Paharganj, New Delhi 110 055 (INDIA)
Tel.: 91-11-2358 0800, 2358 1100, 2358 1300, 2358 3100
Fax: 91-11-2358 0471 • Email: info@bjain.com
Website: www.bjainbooks.com

Printed in India by
J.J. Offset Printers

ISBN: 978-81-319-0293-6

PREFACE

Ever since my teens I always had a keen interest in he paranormal sciences and the energies of universe and became aware of the forces that silently inspired me. In this process I learned so much about Universal energies that I wanted to enlighten the world and let them know that magic is everywhere and in everything that surrounds us and in ourselves too. The spells can boost your confidence and help you harness your own spiritual energy to the fullest potential. The rituals can open doors and bring you opportunities that you otherwise might never have known about. This book is the brainchild of my knowledge of universal energies and the various creative ways to reawaken its powers along with the traditional spells that have always been a guide for weaving good magic. With this book people from every walk of life from the busy housewives to the high flying executives can practice these easy and fun enchantments. With patience and practice, they can benefit to gain more control over their life to start making it happen the way they always wanted it to, rather than leaving it to destiny. So, whether you are looking for a spell of love, luck and prosperity, here's an enjoyable but effective way to ensure your stay on the good side of Lady Luck, always! The best part? There are ways to make it happen.

I sincerely hope this book "Just Spells" would provide all my readers with some easy to do remedial measures, affirmations and fengshui tips that could spice up their life.

BHAVANA SHARMA

www.tarotmystic.com

Email:bhuvi000@yahoo.com

bhuvi00004@gmail.com

ABOUT THE AUTHOR

 BHAVANA SHARMA is an intuitive Tarot Card Reader and Rune Stone Reader with profound interest in color therapy and crystal healing. She has in-depth knowledge of universal energies and the various ways to reawaken them with the different spells that have been a guide for weaving good magic.

As an individual she was always inclined towards the unknown, and a workshop in Occult studies in Sydney helped her to take the plunge. She has keen interest in the esoteric world of tarot and helps people gain insights to guide them in their daily lives. The author has written for many publications from time to time and her interest in mysticism has fuelled her to write this book "Just Spells".

ACKNOWLEDGEMENT

I express my sincere gratitude to journalist Anuradha Varma for giving me this wonderful opportunity to write this book. Special thanks to B.Jain Publishers for their commitment, patience and encouragement and to Dr Geeta Rani Arora and Dr Shruti Kirti Goel for their guidance and to all others who assisted greatly with the technical process. Without these people this book would never have seen the light of day, so I am eternally grateful.

BHAVANA SHARMA

FOREWORD

"I have enjoyed going through the pages of this book. It spells just right! It will help you create a balance, awaken your emotional awareness and why not light a candle that Bhavana has suggested in this book. Don?t forget to add the flowers which will brighten up the path that you are seeking."

Nafisa Ali
Social Activist

"This is a readable book of little prayers, rather than spells, enhanced with candlelight and fragrances to invite healing cosmic energies !"

Ma Prem Usha

CONTENTS

HEALTH, HOME AND HARMONY SPELLS

FINANCE AND FORTUNE SPELL

MISCELLANEOUS SPELLS

INTRODUCTION

Humans have always had a great and deep respect for fire and its power. It was not long before that they discovered that fire had always two aspects the sacred and the mundane. They started to make use of the fire in a sacred way by performing Spells through incantation and making charms. Thus the so called traditional Spells that we have today came into practice. Today's generation believe in spiritual healings and want to dwell on the deepest of New age therapies to rediscover a spiritual dimension in their lives. Mediums like the Candle Spells, affirmations and Fengshui practices are comforting and bring positive results. But to achieve success through Candle Spells and affirmations you should have a strong will power and a deep desire to achieve your goal. You cannot halfheartedly do the rituals -it will not work. You must be determined to achieve the result and be totally engrossed in it at that moment - body, mind, emotions and spirit. If the goal is difficult to manifest, you may have to repeat the spell over a period of time to sustain the effects in the proper phases of the moon. So to ensure the best probability of success for your Candle rituals you should time them to correspond with certain phases of the moon namely waxing (the time when moon is increasing) and waning (the time when moon is decreasing). The idea behind this is that you are connecting with a stronger energy for use in your Spells. The waxing cycle of the moon draws in stronger and positive energies towards your Spells. So during the waxing moon you can perform spellwork for beginning all positive projects, prosperity, growth, love and success. Likewise the waning moon cycles is generally used for banishing negativity, protection and terminating unhealthy relationships.

Again, each day of the week traditionally is connected with a specific planet, so certain Spells should be performed on a particular day only. We should also note that the planetary colors and their powers also have a special effect on the Spells .So different color Candles have to be used on the appropriate days to call upon the energy and invoke them. The types of Candles to be used may be taper or votive Candles. Do not use tea-light colored Candles or scented Candles for your Spells. Along with this the use of certain specific incense, oils and crystals form a very important part of the Spell. They add psychic energy to your work and help you to concentrate more deeply on your ritual. You can choose the crystals in their natural state or tumbled and this can be as effective as expensive ones.

So, whether you need to get your offices reverberating with positive chi or you are hitting at having harmonious relations with your family, or a loved one, the book offers simple suggested solution which includes meditation in the "aura" of some specifically colored Candles and more...So read on...

All rituals are to be done at the readers own risk and author is not responsible for any consequences arising thereof.

RELATIONSHIP SPELLS

LOOK AT MY EYES

REQUIREMENTS:

A STRAIGHT WOODEN STICK
A KNIFE
TWO GREEN RIBBONS
TWO YELLOW RIBBONS
A THREAD OF WOOL
BEADS
PENDANTS OR STONES FOR DECORATION

Now take the lengths of the ribbon and tie them up around the top of the stick using the thread or wool. Hold the stick tightly and pull out the ribbons on either side. Then weave the ribbons together at the end of the stick, overlapping each other. Secure the ends with thread. You can tie pendants, beads or stones on them as decoration. When your wand is ready, hold it in your hand and chant the following words:

"Let the flow of softness and delight in my heart create positive energy of unconditional love in myself and others."

PLEASE A LOVED ONE OR
FOR BUDDING ROMANCES

You know how romantic it is to send or receive long-stemmed red roses. Red roses are a universal expression of romantic love. To send flowers to loved ones, select yellow ones. These signify yang energy as well as the wonderful subdued energy of the earth. When sending flowers to your lover, always send those that contain fresh young leaves to indicate growth in relationships. They also contain chi energy, which is most auspicious for budding romances or for bringing fresh vigor into a marriage that has become stale and stagnant.

PLAY THE CHIC GODDESS

REQUIREMENTS:

WHITE CANDLE

LAVENDER OIL

To help soften the severity of emotional pain so that your experiences do not feel as devastating, you can light a white candle and smudge it with lavender oil and say the following lines:

"I help to redirect my energies to a more balanced state, rather than being an observer where experiences happen to me".

You can repeat this process as many times as you like during the day.

PINK AT HEART

This spell can be used to bring back an ex-lover or end an argument between friends. This ritual should be performed only in the morning.

REQUIREMENTS:

> TWO PINK CANDLES
>
> A PHOTO OR DRAWING OF YOUR LOVER OR FRIEND. (MAKE SURE THAT HE /SHE IS ALONE IN THE PICTURE.)
>
> A PHOTO OF YOURSELF SMILING.

As you sit down for the ritual, light the two pink candles, and keep the photographs by the side of the candle facing downwards. As you focus on the candle say the following words:

"Spirit of the Sun, Spirit of the Sun,
Come today and light the way.
Lend me your power of light,
That it may easily attract my friends/or lover
Back into my life forever, and for the good of all."

DREAM LOVER

Fed up of being single, you can try a new spell to work wonders for you. But, do remember that you shouldn't take anybody's name as this goes against the will of the universe.

REQUIREMENTS:

- TWO GREEN CANDLES
- ROSE PETALS
- CINNAMON INCENSE

Light the candle as you sit to cast your spell, just sprinkle the rose petals around the candle and burn the incense.

As you focus on the candle, say the following words:

"I see my emotional body as holding the key to maintaining balance and wellness, as I also value my emotional sensitivity, knowing that it is all right to feel what I am feeling.

I ask that I may share my love with another who will come to me of his/her free will and together we shall know the beauty of a loving union. I ask this for the highest good of all concerned."

Snuff the candle, and continue doing the same every evening till the universe answers your prayers.

ALONE AT LAST

This is a traditional spell and can be done through simple visualization. You can sit in a quiet room all by yourself and start visualizing that your lover is standing with you in the beauty of nature. As you do this, say this to yourself quietly that though once you were bound together with love and goodwill, you would now like to choose a different path and cast off the ties of this union.

You could ask the universe that you would like to live independent separate lives by saying:

"However bittersweet the parting would be.
Let my heart and soul be free. So mote it be."

REVERBERATING WITH POSITIVE CHI

REQUIREMENTS:

IVY PLANT

JADE PLANT

If you are aiming at having harmonious relations with your co-staff, keep an ivy plant on the eastern sector of your desk. It will build up your expression of constancy and patience. You can also place a small jade plant in the north of the table to boost your wealth prospects and improve business relations.

BANISH A MENTAL FEUD

REQUIREMENTS:

TWO WHITE OR ONE BLUE CANDLE

PHOTOGRAPH OF PERSON WHO HAS HURT

YOUR FEELINGS

Light two white or one blue candle on the night of a New Moon. If you need, keep a photograph of the person who has hurt your feelings. For emotional healing, say the following as you stare at the burning candles:

"What you did has hurt me,
With a pain that burns my heart,
I cleanse myself
From misunderstandings and wish to move on.
Amen."

SPICE UP YOUR LIFE WITH NEW FRIENDS

REQUIREMENTS:

ONE PINK CANDLE

ONE WHITE CANDLE

Our friends are our food of life and good friends are like rare gems, precious and rare. To acquire new friends and spice up your life, you need one pink candle for friendship and one white candle for protection.

As you light the pink candle at dawn, say the following words:

"Venus, light of love, I honor and illuminate your beauty and call upon you to help me with many friends in my life. I call for friends with the same heart that joy and celebration with shall prevail."

Snuff the candles after your spell is done. You could repeat this for seven days until new friends start coming your way.

MAKE SOMEBODY AGREE WITH YOU

REQUIREMENTS:

PINK CANDLE

BLUE CANDLE

Light a pink candle for love and a blue candle for healing on a Friday evening. Say the following incantation:

"Holy light, I request that this person agree with my wishes, and that they reach out for the light of greater wisdom to assist them in changing their beliefs and to act without selfishness."

CHARM A PERSON

REQUIREMENTS:

ONE GOLD CANDLE

SUNFLOWER SEEDS

When you want to charm a person or want to impress somebody you can try this spell and see if it works for you. Light a gold candle and sprinkle some sunflower seeds around it.

As you stare at the flame, say the following words:

"I would like to charm people into my life with goodwill and love. Help me be a source of warmth and light to those I come across. Let me find my powers of magnetic attraction spice up my life and charm people in a magical way."

15

USE LOTUS FOR PURITY IN RELATIONSHIPS

REQUIREMENTS:

LOTUS FLOWER

The Lotus flower is a stunning symbol of purity, so bedrooms and living rooms that are decorated with the lotus plant or flowers, either real or artificial, will nurture a feeling of true peace and contentment in relationships.

ATTRACTING LOVE CHI WITH CRYSTALS

REQUIREMENTS:

QUARTZ CRYSTAL

Place a quartz crystal in the southwest corner of your home, as it will promote harmony and love and actually energize the chi of that area. Look after the crystal and discourage anybody from handling them. You will soon find positive chi being drawn to your home.

IMPROVE RELATIONSHIP WITH YOUR NEAR ONES

REQUIREMENTS:

PASSION FLOWER

DRIED BASIL

Today, brew yourself a tea of a passion flower. Just before drinking, hold the cup in both hands and say:

My heart is open to a path of healing and friendship.

Hold it up to your forehead and say:
Wise ones, help me see how I can bring healing to this relationship.

As you drink the tea, consider how you contribute to the conflict and how you might change your responses. When you expect to be with this person, be sure to carry a small amount of dried basil in your pocket or purse.

A RED GIFT TO ENHANCE MARRIAGE LUCK

The bridegroom should give a gift to his bride, something that represents the fire element and the yang energy. It would be wonderful if he gave her a pair of red shoes, a red evening dress, ruby earrings, cheek blusher, a red bedspread or a pair of bright red planters. The bride can do the same when selecting gifts for her husband. She could buy him a red tie or a silk scarf to ensure marital bliss. She should also buy him a sandalwood fan to express lifelong wishes for fidelity and successful marriage.

RESTORE SPARKLE IN YOUR MARRIAGE

If you wish for the energy between the two of you to sizzle once more, draw symbols of undying love like pairs of geese or mandarin ducks on a banner. Then, write your wish for greater marital bliss. Hang it from your bedroom window and let it catch the wind. The more it flutters in the wind, the more its positive energy is being sent to you. Let it hang for at least seven days and nights before you take it down.

BLESS A NEW RELATIONSHIP

REQUIREMENTS:

FRESH LOAF OF BREAD

Bake a fresh loaf of bread. Hold it up to the moon and ask Our Lady to bless the bread as well as the relationship. Break off a piece of the bread for your partner, as well as one for yourself. As you share time together, share the bread as well. Do not cut the bread with a knife or any other cutting tool. Just break off the pieces with your hands.

MEND A BROKEN HEART

REQUIREMENTS:

ONE BLUE CANDLE

ONE PINK CANDLE

To mend a broken heart, light a blue and a pink candle during the waning moon any day of the week.

As you light it, say the following words:

"Let the past be forgotten, it serves me no more. I evoke the holy flame to release all my sorrows and pain back into the universe, so that my heart can once again feel free to love again.".

RING-A -RING-A ROSES

REQUIREMENTS:
> ONE RED CANDLE
> ONE PINK CANDLE
> RED ROSES
> PINK ROSES

This spell is for securing new relationships. You need a red and pink candle and some red and pink roses. This ritual can be done anytime to bring in the blessings. Sprinkle the rose and pink petals around the candles as you start your spell.

As you light the red candle, say the following words:
"I would like to bring in passion in this relationship."

As you burn the pink candle, stare at the flames and say:
"Bind in the romance in this relationship. May it last forever, and let love and blessings abound."

Your spell is done.

USE A JADE PENDANT TO ATTRACT LOVE

REQUIREMENTS:
JADE STONE

Jade is an ancient love attracting stone. Carved the stone into the shape of a butterfly pendant and wear it to draw love into your life, or you can present it to someone in the hope of obtaining love. You could also use it as an engagement gift and present it to your fiancé. The stone also encourages people around you to let you know you are held in affection. It also works well by encouraging you to love yourself.

FOREVER IN YOUR HEART SPELL

REQUIREMENTS:

Two red strings
Pink sheet of paper
Small rose quartz stones (heart shaped)
Red and pink beads
Pink and red rose petals
Pink heart shaped candle
Rose incense

During the waxing moon, draw a big heart on the pink paper. Fill in the heart with small rose quartz stones (which are heart shaped) and keep the pink candle in the middle of the heart and light it.Put the colorful beads inside and decorate the outline of the heart too. Take the two red strings and tie one end of the string to the other, signifying a bonding between yourself and the person you love. Burn the rose incense stick and as you stare at the flame say the following words:

"Candle of power, Candle of might,
Let my love blossom and stay forever this way.
May no troubles come our way,
Our love shall forever bloom like a red red rose.
For today and always. Amen.
Snuff the candle, and clean up your altar."

HEAL YOURSELF

REQUIREMENTS:
GREEN FLUORITE / JADE CRYSTAL
WHITE CANDLE
A GREEN LEAF

Place the crystals upon the natural green leaf on the table as you light the white candle. For two minutes, meditate looking at the candle and then hold the crystal in your palm. Visualize everyone involved (including yourself) being co-operative and open minded, even if particular persons aren't usually this way. Trust the inner guidance that you receive and know that changes are sometimes uncomfortable but often necessary. In this manner, you can ask the Universe to help with any aspects of relationships that need healing.

It is fine to do this ritual once a day for the complete waning period of the moon.

LOVE CORNER

REQUIREMENTS:

- LOVE BIRDS
- MANDARIN DUCKS
- ORANGE CANDLE
- GARNET CRYSTALS

The southwest corner of your bedroom attracts passionate and romantic love into your life. To make sure that this corner has been activated enough, place love birds and mandarin ducks here for conjugal bliss. To ensure a harmonious relationship between yourself and your lover or spouse, you can also perform a ritual by lighting an orange candle and placing garnet crystals around the candle to bring in yang energy. To complete the spell, allow the orange candle to burn away completely, but making sure that the hot wax does not cause damage in the room. It is fine to repeat this process thrice a week during the waxing moon.

SPIRITUAL LOVE

REQUIREMENTS:

WHITE CANDLE

AMETHYST CRYSTAL

Kindle your spiritual energies with crystals such as amethyst, which can increase your psychic awareness and sharpen sixth sense.

As you light a white candle, hold the amethyst in your hand and ask from the universe to grant you spiritual knowledge and wisdom.

Say the following affirmation:

"Grant me spiritual knowledge and wisdom so that I may use this for good of all mankind. Help me to heighten my spiritual purpose and awareness and connect myself to the Divinity that is within me. Amen."

HAVE A ROCKIN' TIME

If you want to have an active social life, you can try this spell.

REQUIREMENTS:

THREE RED CANDLES

THREE YELLOW CANDLES

THREE ORANGE CANDLES

ONE WHITE CANDLE FOR PROTECTION

FRANKINCENSE AND MYRRH INCENSE

Perform this spell on Friday or Sunday. It is best done during the waxing cycle of the moon.

As you light the candles and burn the incense, say the following:

"The yin and yang energies should come into my life and promote a good social life. May the friends that I gather be drawn to me as I am ready to attract them into my life with love and goodwill. Amen."

It is fine to repeat the spell three times a week during the waxing moon.

FOR BINDING LOVE

REQUIREMENTS:

> Two pink candles
> One pink ribbon
> Rose incense

This spell is best performed for 30 seconds in the evening. During the waxing moon, light the candles and burn the rose incense on your altar, visualizing your lover and yourself. Slowly bring the pink candles together and tie them up with a pink ribbon. Snuff the candles out and repeat the procedure for seven consecutive days.

REMOVING INFIDELITY

REQUIREMENTS:

ONE BLACK CANDLE
ONE WHITE CANDLE
ROSE INCENSE

This is an infidelity spell to protect yourself against unforeseen circumstances. So, if you are married it is a good idea to safeguard against this by ensuring that nothing goes wrong.

As you light the white candle and burn the incense, during the waning moon phase, say the following:

"White candle! Please hear my plea, help me to remove any obstacles in my relationship, in the area of love and friendship and fidelity."

Next, light the black candle and say:
"Hear my plea, help me so that we are not harmed nor alarmed, and that we never go our separate ways, and banish all negativity from our relationship. Amen."

TO ENERGISE YOUR LOVE CORNER

REQUIREMENTS:

RED AND YELLOW CANDLES

RED LANTERNS

LOVE BIRDS

CLEAR QUARTZ CRYSTAL

A PICTURE OF MOUNTAINS

When you have decided the love corner of your home, probably in the southwest corner of your home, you should put red lanterns in this area and burn red and yellow candles to bring in yang energy. You could also place paired images of love birds here as well as place a clear quartz crystal. Hang some pictures of mountains to support the earth energy of your room.

TO WIN BACK A LOVED ONE

REQUIREMENTS:

FOUR RECTANGULAR MIRRORS

YOUR PICTURE

PICTURE OF YOUR LOVED ONE

THICK RED THREAD/RIBBON

Take four rectangular mirrors and stick your picture at the back of one of the mirrors. Take another picture of your loved one with whom you quarreled or had misunderstandings. Stick it behind the other rectangular mirror. Now take the other two mirrors and stick them together back to back, with the mirrored surfaces facing outwards. Now place the pictures on either side of the centre mirrors so that they are facing each other.

You can tie together all the mirrors with a thick red thread or ribbon.

Keep them inside your cupboard for seven consecutive days, after which you could either call or talk to that person with whom you had differences. You are sure to get a positive response and the status quo would be restored soon.

33

SPELL FOR LASTING ROMANCE

REQUIREMENTS:

TWO RED CANDLES
ONE WHITE CANDLE
ONE PINK CANDLE
ROSE INCENSE
ROSE QUARTZ CRYSTAL

On the days of the waxing moon, once a day, light all the colored candles in a straight line on your altar table and place the rose quartz crystal between the red and pink candle. Burn a rose incense to energise your prayers and say the following:

"I identify with lasting love, that which has no beginning and no end. Amen."

CHOOSE BETWEEN LOVERS

REQUIREMENTS:

TWO ROSE

QUARTZ CRYSTALS

Cast this spell on the first crescent of the waxing moon on any day of the week. Keep two rose quartz on the palm of either hand and visualize it in the magical glow of the moonlight. Take the name of your two suitors or lovers and let each crystal represent prospective suitors. Close your palm as well as your eyes for a second. Let your thought flow as you visualize your area of enquiry, the left quartz being for one suitor and the right for the other.

Next, open your eyes and hold the crystal in your palm until it is warm. Observe the color and hue of both the rose quartz crystals. The one which has a darker pinkish hue is the answer and he or she will be the lover or suitor whom you should keep and let go of the other.

Since the solution lies in your subconscious, the answer may also reveal itself to you in your dreams.

SWEET DREAMS

REQUIREMENTS:

MOONSTONE CRYSTAL

Work this spell on a waxing phase of the moon, after moonrise to enhance lunar powers, feelings and dreams. The day should be Monday, dedicated to the Moon Goddess.

Before you go to sleep, mentally picture your angel holding a bucket. You could put all your troubles in that basket and the angel will take it away. Also keep a moonstone crystal under your pillow every night for sweet dreams.

I WANT TO FALL IN LOVE

REQUIREMENTS:

TWO PINK CANDLES

ONE RED CANDLE

ROSE INCENSE

This is a spell you can easily perform by yourself on a waxing moon or on the blue moon day. Light two pink candles and one red candle as well as some rose incense. Breathe deeply and place yourself before the altar.

Visualize yourself falling in love with the person of your choice as you say:
"Lunar lady, bring to me the man or woman of my choice, somebody who is worthy of me."

Your wish should be fulfilled in just one lunar cycle. If not, it is fine to repeat this spell, especially on a new moon day when the new cycle begins.

PASSION PLAY

REQUIREMENTS:

> ONE PURPLE CANDLE
> ONE RED CANDLE

You can cast this spell on a full moon or on a waxing phase. Light a purple and a red candle as this sends out hues of a more earthly kind to speed up your passion.

As you stare at the candle flame on your altar, say:

"My sensuality will make my partner feel special and with my deep understanding I can achieve total commitment. I want my energies to be passionate and sublime."

Visualize your lover and yourself being passionate as ever, sophisticated and feeling cherished.

GET THE ATTENTION OF SOMEONE YOU FANCY

REQUIREMENTS:

PANSY FLOWERS (OF ALL COLORS)

GLASS BOWL

TWO MINT LEAVES

SAGE LEAVES

WHITE CANDLES

WHITE CLOTH

WATER

When you want to get the attention of someone you fancy, collect pansy flowers of all colors and place them in a glass bowl filled with water. Also put two mint leaves into it. This spell has to be carried out during the waxing moon.

As you light the white candles, say the following words:
"I invoke the Moon Goddess to warm their heart towards me and that I appear beautiful in their eyes."

As you put the mint leaves into the water, ask the following:

"Draw his/her eyes towards me and joy to him/her who notices me."

Place the bowl of water in the moonlight for about an hour. Then drain the water out and take the flower petals, sage leaves and tie them in a white cloth and carry it with you the next time you are with your object of affection. Carry this with you till the day of the full moon. If they have not expressed any interest within the one-month moon cycle, repeat the same for the next cycle.

LOVE ENERGISER FOR NORTH-EAST DOORS

REQUIREMENTS:

PINK CANDLE

ROSE INCENSE

If the main door of your home faces north-east you could place a water feature in that sector to activate the positive chi in that area. You could also light a pink candle and facing the north , burn a rose incense and as you look at the flame say "I cleanse, bless and attract love to my house." "Hail to the north wind I call for love and make this offering of light to you."

Say thank you to the elements of Air, Water, Earth and Fire and snuff out the candle.

ROMANTIC BEST

REQUIREMENTS:

TWO PINK CANDLE

ROSE OIL

JADE CRYSTAL

Conduct this ritual on a waxing moon phase by lighting two pink candles and smear them with rose oil.

As you look at the flame, hold a jade crystal and say:

"I want to enjoy beauty, love and the flow of softness and delight in my heart and create positive energy of love in myself and my partner."

You could also carve a jade crystal into the shape of a butterfly and give it to your partner.

HEALTH, HOME AND
HARMONY SPELLS

MAKEOVER MAGIC

REQUIREMENTS:

AN EARTHEN PLATE
SOME FRESH SOIL FROM THE GARDEN
ONE DARK GREEN CANDLE
ONE WHITE CANDLE
SOME SEA SHELLS
SOME STONES

Place the stones and shells around the earthen plate and light the candles on the plate. Then fill the plate with soil.

Look at the burning candle and say:

"I ask for a healthy body and sound mind as I move forward with focus and direction and affirm that every moment is a new beginning."

It is fine to repeat this spell once every week till you feel confident.

45

STRETCH YOUR WORRIES AWAY

REQUIREMENTS:

BLACK CANDLE

Burn a black candle and sit before this and
meditate whenever you feel stressed out. Just pour
out all your negative emotions when you meditate
in front of the black candle, asking it to protect
and bless you. You will soon feel the difference.

DIET-O-HEAL

REQUIREMENTS:

FRESH GREEN LIME

ONE RED CANDLE

This spell improves your dietary habits.
Invoke the powers of fresh green lime fruit to help
you restore health to yourself or another person.

Hold a lime in your hand and light a red candle
and say :

O! healing spirit of the sun,
I light this flame, to honour your presence
And ask you to hear my prayers.
O powers of lime, health is mine,
Cleanse the body, cleanse the mind
And improve my dietary habits,
O! pure spirit fill my (or the persons name) with
health, with health, with health.

REMOVE FEARS

If you don't want to be bogged down with irrational fears, you could try out these rituals and learn to relax the natural way. Visualize and soothe strained nerves by taking an imaginative trip to an ideal place. Or practice positive self-talk, as you will develop a more optimistic outlook on situations and hence lower stress levels by chanting the following words:

"I have the courage and determination to work through all fears, and my mind is relaxed and open to connect with my Higher Guidance."

LET IT SHINE

REQUIREMENTS:

WHITE/ CREAM CANDLE

Sit in a quiet place that is special to you. Hold a
white or cream candle in your hands and visualize
the area of your life where this candle's energy is
needed. Then, light this candle, and imagine the
energy coming to you. It may come right away or
when you least expect it.

Repeat this spell as many times as you like.

FLAUNT A HAPPY LOOK

REQUIREMENTS:

QUARTZ CRYSTAL

If you have a piece of quartz, first wash it in warm soapy water and rinse it with running water. Then hold the crystal in both hands. Close your eyes and imagine being bathed in white light. Visualize the area of your illness and point the crystal to that spot. Imagine a stream of light flowing from the crystal and bathing the area in its pure rays. Place your crystal under your pillow while you sleep.

MOW YOUR CALORIES

REQUIREMENTS:

A MIRROR

On a full moon night take a mirror and stand outside. If you can't, then open a window and make sure the moon is reflected on the mirror.

As you look at the reflection of the moon on the mirror, say the following:

"Light of the night, I see thy reflection and seek help by your moon rays. I ask you to come and bless me, mould my body as a rose is granted beauty and let me grow in your guidance and light. I wish to eat only that which is due to me."

BRIGHT GARDEN LIGHTS TO ATTRACT GOOD CHI

There are some safe and protective ideas to energize your house. Energize your gardens with bright lights at night to attract good chi into your house. This will not only help to keep the flames of love alive between husband and wife, but more excitingly, it can enhance the marriage prospects of all eligible members of the household. The light is thought to represent yang chi, as it entices the chi from inside the earth to rise up. You could also have a cluster of three round lights in your garden somewhere. It is also very auspicious.

WELLNESS IN THE FAMILY

REQUIREMENTS:

LIGHT BLUE CANDLE

If you need to enhance your luck and positive energies, here's how you can use a light blue candle to protect yourself and your family against evil influences and promote harmony in relationships.

At sunrise, place a light-blue candle on your sacred table and as you light it, charge your pledge for this new beginning each day by repeating this affirmation:

"I pledge, dear father, that my affirmations be to work within your service and always to love and respect thee."

Before you leave the room, snuff the candle, and don't forget to continue doing the same every morning for seven consecutive days. You will soon discover how the warm glow of these candle prayers lights up your life!

HEAL A PERSON FROM NEGATIVE ENERGIES

REQUIREMENTS:

WHITE CANDLE (FOR PROTECTION)

GREEN CANDLE

PICTURE OF THE PERSON WHO NEEDS HEALING

Place the picture of the concerned person, between the white & the green candle. As you light the candle, visualize the person in your mind and send them the healing energise by saying the following three times:

"I reach for the light of greater energies to assist me in my healing process.Amen."

Leave the candles to burn for one hour.

GET A WHIFF OF THIS (PROTECTION AND HARMONY)

REQUIREMENTS:

A WHITE CANDLE AND SALT

Place the candle in the middle of the room.
Sprinkle the salt in a circle around the candle.

Light and say:

"Higher energies, give me a sense of protection
and safety,
I am surrounded and protected by light,
The beauty and flexibility of my vibrations
Are such that they can program me to resonate
And enhance the energy already present in this
house."

Leave the candle to burn for at least 1 hour.

IN RHYTHM WITH THE UNIVERSE

REQUIREMENTS:
A WHITE CANDLE
SALT

Place the candle in the middle of the room.
Sprinkle the salt in a circle around the candle.

Light it and say:

"I am emotionally safe and protected
And I want to be in rhythm with the universal
energy"

Leave to burn for at least 1 hour.

CROWNING GLORY

REQUIREMENTS:

ONE PINK CANDLE

MOONSTONE

This spell can be done by all who want to have gorgeous and well-nourished hair. Burn a pink candle, hold a moonstone in your hand and, as you stare at the flame, say the following words:

"Make my hair grow thick and long,
O Goddess, I offer this moonstone in your honour
And ask that you imbue it with your power
To make this wish come true. Amen."

ALL IN GOOD HEALTH

REQUIREMENTS:

GREEN CANDLE

RED CANDLE

To maintain good health, all you have to do is to buy green candles that signify health and fertility, along with red candles for vigor and vitality. Place the red and green candles next to each other and light them. This should be done on Fridays only, during the waning moon. Start your prayers by praying to the God and Goddess. Ask them to bless you with good health. This spell will charge you with positive energy, flush out bad stress and leave you feeling refreshed. Snuff out the candles and thank the Almighty for their presence.

DON'T GAIN WEIGHT

This is a traditional spell to help reduce weight, if followed carefully.

REQUIREMENTS:

A YELLOW CANDLE

LAVENDER OIL

SMALL GARNETS, CARNELIAN OR TURQUOISE STONES

A SMALL JAR WITH A LID OR A PLASTIC BAG THAT SEALS

ROSE PETALS

Charge the yellow candle, by visualizing your desired goal while focusing on the candle. Place it in the holder. As you light the candle, visualize yourself passing second helpings of food onto your plate in small portions and looking healthy and physically fit.

Charge the rose petals, oil and stones.

Sprinkle petals around the candle and again visualize your goal.

Place the charged garnet stones and a few drops of oil into the jar or bag. A small jar used to store baby food might work well. As you do this, repeat the visualization. Then pick up the petals and place them in the jar or bag.

Seal the jar or bag and say:

"By this jar/bag of powered oil, petals and stones, it will bring me courage and help me meet my goal to not eat or snack as much and become healthier."

Visualize yourself becoming healthier and moving the weight on the scale to the left. Carry this jar or bag with you and sniff charged items before eating.
Rub the charged carnelian or turquoise on the picture of yourself, then onto your body while visualizing yourself resembling you in the picture. Carry the stone with you and rub it when you have the urge to snack or eat too much. Hang the picture up in your kitchen to view. Allow the candle to burn for another hour, then snuff it out and put away. Light it whenever you need moral support.

PROTECT YOUR HOME

For protecting your home you could say these words as you close the door of your house. You could also stop a certain person from entering your home. Just recite the following lines while closing the door. If you have a lock on the door, then you should also use it on the door while reciting the passage.

"Guard this threshold,
Guard this door,
So that (person's name),
Can pass no more."

FOUR CORNERS

REQUIREMENTS:

WATER

SAFFRON

THREE INCENSE STICKS

SEVEN TYPES OF AUSPICIOUS FLOWERS

THREE GOLD & SILVER ORNAMENTS

For an excellent ritual that brings harmony to a home, fill a jug of water, mix some saffron in the water and once it has turned yellow, sprinkle it all over the northeast of your home. Again, for the southwest section of your home, light three incense sticks to energize good earth energy in this area of your home. For the southeast section, pluck seven types of auspicious flowers of any colors and sprinkle flower petals to symbolize the power of wealth and prosperity. And for the northwest of your home, place three gold and silver ornaments on a platter. The symbolism of the metal will enhance the chi in this area.

CLEAN SWEEP

REQUIREMENTS:

WATER

SALT

If your home feels like there is something there that shouldn't be, or that someone is thinking ill of you or sending bad vibes your way, try this. Mix salt and water, and bless it.

Go through your home, sprinkling the salt water around, and recite in a loud voice:

"I cleanse and clean this room of all negative vibrations and energies for the good of all. I call upon the gods to bless this house, so that all who enter will also be blessed."

ZAP THAT FLAB

REQUIREMENTS:

ONE RED CANDLE

When you want to control your diet and reduce calories, here is a simple spell that might help you.

You need to burn a red candle on the waning days of the moon and say the following words:

"I am in control of my body and through the help of my higher powers, I will eat what is needed to satisfy my hunger. I can easily make my body healthy and attractive, filled with loving energy."

Snuff the candle out and repeat the same ritual till you feel confident about yourself.

WE ALL ARE ONE

REQUIREMENTS:

BARKS OF WOOD FROM ANY TREE

RED CANDLES

YELLOW CANDLES

SUNFLOWER SEEDS

Domestic harmony is so important in modern day life. We need the peace and sanctuary of home in order to stay healthy and to go out and socialize with ease. So, here is how to cast this spell. Make an altar in the southwest corner of your living room. Place some barks of wood from any tree of your choice. Keep small red and yellow candles there and light them daily for about an hour. You can also sprinkle some sunflower seeds around the candle before you light it. This will enhance the happy disposition among family members and build a good social circle.

TO GAIN SUCCESS

REQUIREMENTS:

ORANGE CANDLE FOR SUCCESS
GREEN CANDLE FOR LUCK
LAVENDER OIL
DEATH TAROT CARD, WHICH REPRESENTS
CHANGE/TRANSITION

The ideal time to perform this spell is during the waxing of the moon. Take a drop of the lavender oil and apply it, starting from the middle of the candle up to the north pole and back to middle. Again, apply the same oil starting from the middle of the candle to the bottom of the candle and back to the middle. First, apply the oil to the orange candle, then follow the same procedure for the green candle. When this is complete, place the candles side by side.

In the middle of the two candles, place the Death card.

Now say these words:

"Please give me the strength to change
Allow me to bring luck where I need it
Give me the success I am seeking
Allow me to do this without loss to myself
Let me remain true to who I am"

Now light both candles. Let them burn completely.
Take the death card and place it in your pocket or
purse and carry it with you until you have feel
confident that you have achieved what you
desired.

67

TO GET RID OF UNWANTED FEARS

REQUIREMENTS:

AMETHYST PYRAMID OR BALL

For this ritual all you need is an amethyst pyramid or ball. As you hold this precious stone in your hand, wish away unwanted fears from your subconscious mind. You can call on your guardian angels or just pray to Archangel Micheal by imagining a circle of bright purple light surrounding your whole body. Visualize this light repelling all lower energies such as fear away from your mind and attracting loving energies towards yourself.

GIVE YOUR CARES AWAY

REQUIREMENTS:

> MALACHITE CRYSTALS
> EMERALD CRYSTALS
> SEA SALT WATER

For this spell you require the healing crystals of malachite and emerald. Soak the crystals in a cup of sea salt water overnight. In the morning, throw the water away and hold the crystals in your hand under running tap water. The crystals are ready for sending your affirmations into the universe. Next, close your eyes, hold the crystals in the palm of your hand and take a deep cleansing breath. Then mentally call upon your guardian angels to remove your cares and worries away. Try to imagine healing yourself with the emerald green aura you hold in your palm.

It is fine to do this twice a day as you get gradually aligned with the universal energy and allow the cosmic energy to take away your cares and burdens.

RESET YOUR BODY RHYTHM

REQUIREMENTS:

AMETHYST CRYSTAL

ONE WHITE AND ONE PURPLE CANDLE

ROSE INCENSE

For this spell, you can practice relaxation methods such as yoga, deep breathing and meditation. Next, as you sit down to start your prayers, hold the amethyst crystal in the palm of your hand, light the white and purple candles along with the rose incense and visualize your life in the most beautiful way you can imagine. Manifest your dreams by actually sending out positive thoughts to the universe.

You can say the affirmation:
"I am the master ocean of peace, I am the master ocean of love, bring to me victory and success."

ENERGISE THE EARTH
SECTORS OF YOUR HOME

REQUIREMENTS:

ONE BLUE CANDLE
ONE WHITE CANDLE
FRANKINCENSE
A MAGICAL SYMBOL - A STAR OR ANY
   GEMSTONE (PREFERABLY AN AMETHYST)

Perform this spell to energize the earth corners of your home. Light the candles alongwith the incense, in the south west corner on the days when the moon is waxing.

As you stare at the flame, say the following:

"Mother Earth, you bring things together and symbolize the physical body and all good things of life. Energize, nurture and protect us all and the earth corner of my home so that we have stability, cohesion and the power to manifest in the material world all what is due to us. Give us your blessings in business and career matters and where our inner strength, stamina and patience are called for. Amen."

AID COMMUNICATION

REQUIREMENTS:
    COLORED PAPER STREAMERS
    ONE YELLOW CANDLE
    ONE FEATHER QUILL PEN
    A BOTTLE OF RED INK
    LAVENDER INCENSE

This spell is specially to aid better communication between people who are perhaps drawn to each other.

Begin your ritual during the waxing moon on Wednesday, sacred to Mercury, God of communication. With a quill pen dipped in red ink write your name on one side of the streamer and your partners on the other side. Repeat the same in about, at least, six colored steamers. Tie them up like a chain. Write words on it like talk, speak, listen, give, receive, look, trust, etc - all aids in effective communication.

As you light the candle, say the following words: "I want to grow through effective communication with those whom I like."

Make a chain of the same and hang them up in your room.

FINANCE AND
FORTUNE SPELLS

REMOVE OBSTACLES AT WORK

REQUIREMENTS:

SOME BASIL SEEDS
ONE BLACK CANDLE
ONE TEASPOON OF SESAME OIL
SOME DRIED GRASS
A PLATE MADE OF MUD

If you have been trying hard to get a promotion, but have been feeling rather frustrated recently, it's good to try out this spell and see that opportunities spring up your way.

This spell should be done during the waning moon. Prepare your altar by placing the black candle in the center of the mud plate. Sprinkle some small dried grass around the candle. Add one drop of sesame oil and mix it with the dried grass.
Before you light the black candle, burn some basil leaves to remove the negative vibrations away.

As you look at the flame of the candle, say the following:

"I hereby desire that all negativity and obstacles be cleared from my work path.

Hindrances of any kind be out of my way. Oh, mighty candle, remove all blocks and let me see my way."

Repeat this three times before the black candle and visualize all obstacles moving away.

PROSPERITY SPELL

REQUIREMENTS:

WHITE CANDLES

To activate your luck and gain prosperity, gather your thoughts gently. Take several slow breaths, and when you feel composed, write down exactly what you want in terms of prosperity in your life. Do you want to find a husband to share your life with, a wife to start a family, someone to love you? Think through what you want very carefully and then write it down clearly. Try to be brief but as clear as you can. Now keep the paper in front of a white candle, and pray to the universe to grant your wishes.

SELL-WELL

REQUIREMENTS:

YELLOW FLOWERS

YELLOW CANDLE

PHOTOGRAPH OF THE ITEM YOU WANT TO SELL

Whenever you have anything to sell, whether it's something really big like a car or house, you can perhaps try this spell and see how you can succeed.

Buy some yellow flowers and burn a yellow candle to start with. Place a photograph of the item you want to sell in front of the yellow candle and put some yellow flowers around it.

As you stare at the candle flame, say the following words:

"I would want to let go of this article, so that something new may come its way. May it happen and I receive money in return. This is for the highest good of all concerned."

INCREASE YOUR BUSINESS CALLS

REQUIREMENTS:

PIECE OF PARCHMENT OR FINE QUALITY WRITING PAPER

Take a piece of parchment or fine quality writing paper and inscribe the name of the target. Write it in a circle twice, so the ends meet. As you do this, concentrate on the person's face and your desire of business coming to you.

BUSINESS PROTECTION

REQUIREMENTS:

BOWL OF CANDIES, HERBS OR STONES

To bless your home or business, place a bowl of candies, herbs or stones by your front entrance.

Bless the bowl's contents by speaking aloud the following verse:

As all who enter here are children of the Great
Mother,
May those who pass always walk safely in her
steps.
May they feel the guidance of her hand,
And know she is always with us,
From the time we meet till we meet again.

Invite visitors to take an offering as they enter the premises.

JACKPOT

REQUIREMENTS:

FOUR-LEAFED CLOVER

SOME RUPEE NOTES & COINS

CINNAMON INCENSE

PERIDOT STONE

GREEN CANDLE

The next time you buy a lottery ticket, you can better your chances of winning the jackpot! So, here we go.

After you purchase the ticket, place it on a table along with a four-leafed clover, some rupee notes and coins. You can burn cinnamon incense and place a peridot stone as well on your table. Light a green candle, and visualize the money coming to you. As you stare at the flame also chant the following words "Rich I will be, money and power come hither to me." Snuff out the candle and repeat the same for three days.

BRING IN OPPORTUNITIES

REQUIREMENTS:

AMBER CRYSTAL

Hold an amber crystal in your hand as you send out affirmations into the universe by saying:

"I hope to gain more opportunities in the future, to prepare for change through gradual adjustment so that there is a sense of safety and reassurance. Help me to bring in myriad opportunities with my prayers. Amen."

HARMONY AT THE WORKPLACE

REQUIREMENTS:
- ROSE PETALS
- LAVENDER OIL
- ROSE OIL
- SANDALWOOD OIL
- TALCUM POWDER
- BLUE CANDLE
- EARTHEN POT
- BASIL LEAVES
- DRIED GRASS

When your office atmosphere gets stressful, here is a simple spell you can try out to make the atmosphere peaceful. Take rose petals and mix two drops of lavender oil, rose oil, sandalwood oil and a handful of talcum powder. Mix these together in a bowl, until the petals are crushed completely and well blended. Put the powder in a sachet and keep it ready for your spell.

Next, burn a blue candle in an earthen pot and add basil leaves and dried grass to it and light using a lighter.

As you look at the flames of the candle as well as the earthen pot, sprinkle the powder of crushed rose petals and say the following:

"I pray for harmony and peace at my workplace, with harm to none, so mote it be."

FORTUNE FINDER

REQUIREMENTS:

ORANGES

It is a good idea to lavishly display oranges in the home during festivals, New Year celebrations and even on a wedding day. Oranges are regarded as being a fruit that signifies gold, which in turn is another word for "good fortune". So, here's a quick and easy way to activate your fortune. While throwing the succulent oranges into the river, close your eyes and make a wish, and let the waters carry the oranges into the great unknown, as you visualize all the happiness in this world coming to you. It is fine to repeat this practice for a few days.

MISCELLANEOUS SPELLS

TURN THE CLOCK AROUND

REQUIREMENTS:

SEVEN BLUE CANDLES

To perform the following wishing spell, you will need seven blue candles. Write your wish on each of the seven candles.
Burn the candles and say:

"Dear Goddess, as I light my candle grant that all my wishes come true, as I am open to all the greater possibilities."

You can say this seven times, and then snuff the candle. This spell can be done every time you want to wish for something.

BIRTHDAY WISH
REQUIREMENTS:
PAPER
PEN
F͟͟ RING PLANT

n your birthday, write your wish on a piece of paper and keep it under a flowering plant or plant a seed and put your wish there. It will grow and manifest.

PROTECTION FROM ENEMY

If you are feeling uneasy, nervous or threatened, try repeating this chant quietly to yourself:

"I have courage and determination to work through all fears, and to be who I truly am."

GAIN CONFIDENCE

REQUIREMENTS:

    A SHELL TO ACT AS A LUCKY CHARM

    YELLOW CANDLE

This spell has to done during the waxing moon, preferably on a Friday.

As you light the candle, hold it in your right hand and say:

"Please give me confidence to be at my best, having failed once, I shall do better this time."

Pass the shell through the candle flames and say:

"This should be a lucky charm to me,
I shall carry it with me,
My wishes shall all come true,
And may it help me in whatever I set out to do."

SEEK HELP

REQUIREMENTS:

YELLOW CANDLE

You may be using this spell to get a promotion at work, or a pay rise or simply for your friends to take more notice of you.

To seek help, burn a yellow candle and as you look at the flame, meditate and ask the universe to answer your wishes by saying the following words:

"I seek the truth in understanding my experiences. Empower me, as I ask this favor, please help me to shine in whatever I do, and to receive fitting rewards for my efforts."

Blow out the candle and give thanks to the Universe.

TREE MAGIC

REQUIREMENTS:

AMETHYST STONE

OAK TREE

In this spell, you will discover the magical properties of trees. You can perform this whenever you are leaving something behind and starting something new. This can be anything from starting exams, to a new job or moving house. Go near a tree, specially an oak tree and tell it your intentions. Place a small amethyst at its base as an offering.

Walking around the tree, say the following:

"I ask you, dear oak tree, to hear my call, light my path, guide my actions, words and thoughts and those of all I am yet to meet, that by the power of your might, all will be fortunate to my sight."

Next, visualize yourself being surrounded by the arms of the great oak tree. Now, take the amethyst stone, place it in a bag and say the words:

"Heart of oak, you are my heart with honor, I shall carry you by my side. Thank you."

Carry the stone with you whenever you meet with new opportunities.

GET CLEAR VISION

REQUIREMENTS:

ONE WHITE CANDLE

LAVENDER OIL

The path of life is never straightforward. With so many options, we find it hard to make a choice. If you can't see the way ahead, call upon the Goddess to gain some clarity.

Find a comfortable place to sit and do the ritual. Burn a white candle and smudge some lavender oil on it.

As you stare at the flame, close your eyes and invoke the good spirit of nature by saying:

"I call upon you, Mother Nature and Goddess. Speedily, come now, and assist me in my life's decisions. Please lend me your power, so that I may see the way ahead clearly."

Repeat this whenever you find yourself in a crisis or at crossroads while taking decisions.

FIND WHAT IS LOST

REQUIREMENTS:

ONE BLUE CANDLE

During the waning moon, light a blue candle and concentrate on your need to find what had been lost, and chant the following:

"I desire to find what I have lost,
Lead me on to the road I seek
Reveal a clue and show me the way."

Blow out the candle and give thanks to the universe for helping you in your quest.

LOOK BEAUTIFUL

REQUIREMENTS:

- SOME PINK ROSES
- RED ROSES
- STREAMERS
- HAT
- RED & PINK CANDLES
- ROSE INCENSE STICK

Cut the colored streamers and decorate the straw hat with it. Place pink and yellow colored petals all around the hat.

Now, place the decorated straw hat on your altar and light the red and pink candle along with a rose incense stick.

Look at the brightly colored straw hat, which represents beauty, and say the following words:

"Pretty and decorated straw hat, my desire is to look beautiful and charming, as I want to be reflected in your glory."

As you look at the flame, allow the candle to burn out completely.

TAKE GRIEF AWAY FROM ME
REQUIREMENTS:

SMOKY QUARTZ CRYSTAL

THREE TABLESPOONS OF SEA SALT

For this spell, all you need is smoky quartz crystal and three tablespoons of sea salt. Wash the stone in water by adding the sea salt to it. Begin by holding the stone in your hand as you visualize the grief moving away from your mind.

As you visualize this, say the following lines:

"My purpose is to uproot the grief which I feel in my mind and that I become happy, bold and dynamic. I sense the importance of starting fresh and would like to initiate new ways of thinking. I am now free of grief as I expand beyond perceived limitations from my past."

LUCKY FRIENDSHIP SPELL

REQUIREMENTS:

- PAPER
- APPLE
- PINK CANDLE WAX

If you want to make a positive wish for being lucky and joyful in your friend circle, here is what will help you do so. Write on a piece of paper your wish for acquiring new friends in the future and place the paper in a half cut apple. Seal with a pink candle wax and bury it in the soil somewhere near the house. If the apple seeds grow, tend them carefully because they represent new friendships and success in existing relationships.

I CONTROL MYSELF

REQUIREMENTS:

CALCITE CRYSTAL

SALT WATER

Making magic is really about your will-power, focusing to achieve whatever you want. All you have to do is to hold a calcite crystal in your hand after washing it with salt water and say the following lines when you feel the need to control your mind in certain adverse circumstances.

"I release all tension and feel calm and relaxed, in full control of my situation. I have a peaceful sense of being in control of myself and my experiences. I would not follow any overly volatile approach in any aspect of my life."

You can repeat this process whenever there is a need to calm and control yourself.

GET THE RIGHT ATTITUDE

REQUIREMENTS:

ONE WHITE CANDLE

When you need to have the right attitude, burn a white candle and as you stare at the flame, repeat this in your mind three times.

"Candle of protection, Candle of power,
Open my mind like a growing flower
And empower my vision with right attitude,
Open the gates, that I may roam
And strengthen my aura in positive ways."

BOOST YANG ENERGY

REQUIREMENTS:

RED LIGHT

RED CANDLE

YELLOW CANDLE

The sun yang increases energy in the house, bringing about improvements in all aspects of one's life. Place red lights in the southwest corner of any room. Along with this, you could also burn a red and yellow candle to boost the yang energy in that corner.

REMOVE NEGATIVITY WITH MOON YIN

REQUIREMENTS:

CRYSTALS

The best way to bring moon yin energy into your house is by buying crystals and placing them under the light of the moon on a full moon night. This ensures that they are bathed and charged with moon yin chi. Bring them back and place them in all corners of your house. By placing these highly charged moon yin crystals, any lingering negative energies like anger caused by household disagreements, negative minded visitors and occasional temper tantrums will be removed from the house. You will soon find that your family social circle is positive and rewarding.

CHIRP OUT THE BLUES

When you are stuck in a rut, just go out and buy yourself a new houseplant. You can do this when you get the sense that you are surrounded by stale energy. Most people can easily pick up on this kind of vibe - emotionally, you might be feeling stuck, bored, frustrated or discouraged. This stale energy also often manifests itself on the physical plane - the phone never rings, your loved ones and pets seem irritable, and the bills arrive long before you collect the money to pay them.

When you find yourself stuck in a chronic pattern, it usually means that your personality has somehow temporarily disconnected from your higher self. The traditional quick fix for reconnecting to your higher self would be to spend some time in nature. It is my personal opinion, that a half an hour spent in nature by a stream or pool can do more for your body or soul. However, once you come back home, you might find yourself drawn low emotionally and spiritually by the dull and oppressive vibes hanging around in your environment. The spiritual remedy for this is to bring a little bit of nature back inside to try and raise the vibrations in your home. Plants naturally have a connection to the higher realms that you can access just by having them in your energy field.

GET WHAT YOU WANT

REQUIREMENTS:

HORSESHOE
RED CANDLE
QUILT PEN
BLACK INK

Take a horseshoe and put it around a red candle.
Place the candle in a darkened room in the middle
of a table. Write what you want on a piece of
paper with a quill pen dipped in black ink.
Chant the following as you write:

"What I want I write here
Please take my dream and bring it near
What I want is what I should get
Let all my dreams
Now be met"

Now, take the paper and fold it in a square of four
creases. Hold it over the candle with a pair of
tweezers and let it burn. Picture yourself with your
wish fulfilled as you burn the paper. Send waves of
love at the image you conjure of yourself. There's
only one catch to this spell... watch what you ask
for!

RING IN THE NEW YEAR
REQUIREMENTS:
- AMETHYST STONE
- QUARTZ CRYSTAL
- SEA SALT
- CANDLE

Get an amethyst stone and quartz crystal and boil 3 cups of water. Add 1 teaspoon of sea salt. When the water is cool, pour it over the amethyst stone and crystal points. Let the stone and points dry in sunlight. If you can't put them outside you can place them in a window where the sun will shine on them. To give extra strength to the ritual, clean your home before performing it. As you clean, think that you are "sweeping out the old negativity". Bathe with your favorite soap or bath gel. Dress in dark colored clothes. Place the amethyst stone, quartz crystal points, sea salt, candle and holder, matches, bag and put in a basket or bag and carry them in your right hand to the room where you spend the most time in your home. This can be the living room, den, kitchen, bedroom or any other room that you use most often. Take the items out of the basket with your left hand and place them on a table.

As you light the candle, say:

I light the fire that burns the old

Take a pinch of sea salt in your right hand and toss
it over your left shoulder and say:

With this salt I banish negativity
Take the amethyst stone in your left hand and say:
Flow to me abundance

Place the amethyst stone where you will see it
often. Take both of the quartz crystal points in
your left hand and say:

I HOLD ABUNDANCE
I HOLD HEALTH
I HOLD LOVE
I HOLD HAPPINESS

Put 1 crystal quartz point in the southern most
corner of the room put the other point in the bag.
Keep it with you or put it somewhere safe.
Let the candle burn out. Now begin that
wonderful life you deserve! This may be repeated
every three months to reinforce the good life.

WELL-BEING SPELL

REQUIREMENTS:

WHITE CANDLE

You can burn a white candle and as you stare at the flame to meditate, say the following words:

"I work more broadly with my energy system to help myself focus or center that which is most appropriate to me at that moment. I effectively ground the energies that are being transmitted from outside for my well-being. I thereby integrate my spiritual awareness by establishing my priorities and acting upon them."

REAL BLISS

REQUIREMENTS:

THREE ORANGE CANDLES

As you light the candles, focus on the elements of your life that bring you stress and visualize them fading away and leaving only peace and happiness in your heart. Repeat the words below several times. Say out loud all the things that make you happy, no matter how small they are.

The words to be said are:
"Happiness and joy should come into my life in abundance. Away with all stress and anger. I am happy, I am free and I shall continue to be."

BAG IT ALL
REQUIREMENTS:
TWO SMALL EQUAL PIECES OF RED CLOTH
RED WOOLEN THREAD
A CRUMB OF BREAD
A PINCH OF SALT

Sew three of the four sides of red cloth together with the red woolen thread. Turn the bag outside in because it should have been inside out when you were sewing it. Put the crumb of bread, the pinch of salt, and sew it up.

Say this chant for good fortune:

This bag I sew for luck for me, and also for my family
That it may keep by night and day, troubles and illness far away.

Hang the bag over your bed, your window, or keep it in your purse.

RIGHT ATTITUDE

REQUIREMENTS:

STONE (ALMOST SQUARE IN SHAPE)

ONE WHITE CANDLE

Many times in our life, we fail because we do not have the right attitude towards life and circumstances. In order to find the ingredients for this spell, you have to go out into the garden and pick up a stone that is almost square in shape. Go by your instincts and if the stone feels good as you hold it, use it for your spell. Write on one side of the stone your desire to have the right attitude towards everything in life. Burn a white candle and keep the stone near it.

As you gaze at the candle flames and the stone, ask the stone to grant your wish by saying:

"I affirm the power of my perseverance to see me through all situations. I reflect inner certainty, as I speak with non-judgment and discernment. Help me to have the right attitude towards myself and others."

Snuff out the candle and carry the stone in your bag at all times. It is fine to repeat this spell as and when required.

ATTRACT LUCK IN YOUR LIFE

On a full moon day, go out into the open and look at the moon.

Say the following words:

"Dear Moon Goddess! Lady of Luck,
Thy power and beauty is known to all,
Come, heed my prayers,
Bless me and shed thy light upon me,
And bless me so that I am lucky
In everything that I set out to do
I thank thee mother with all my heart."

SOUNDS OF SILENCE

REQUIREMENTS:

ONE BLUE CANDLE

ONE WHITE CANDLE

ONE YELLOW CANDLE

CINNAMON INCENSE

When you want to find inner peace, light a blue, white and yellow candle during the waxing moon. As you light all three candles, also burn an incense of cinnamon. Just meditate as you stare at the flame and say the following words:

"Please help me to bring calmness, primarily at my mental level, and extending this to whatever I verbally express with others. Help me to slow and still my mind and that there is no wasted energy through the impulsive expression of my irrelevant thoughts. I want to receive guidance and emotional calmness so that it allows me to open up to new experiences."

GET ARTY

All you need is to first decide what you want from this universe. On the new moon day, write out your desires and paste pictures of what you want out of life on a scrapbook. Be careful what you ask for, for it shall manifest.

You can even take a brush and paint whatever you decide to get during this new moon period.

But, before you decide to paint, repeat these words three times:

"As I start my painting, my spell has begun.
As I continue to paint my wishes should come true."

When you are finished with your work of art, paste it in your scrapbook, and wait for your wishes to manifest.

BON VOYAGE

REQUIREMENTS:

PENDULUM

This is a fairly easy spell and can be used by anybody who would like to know whether it is the safe time to travel.

Hold a pendulum in your hand and ask of it the direction for your journey. If the pendulum swings to the right, it indicates that the journey could be undertaken safely. But if it swings to the left, it indicates some impending danger and that the journey should hence be delayed.

CAR PROTECTION

Before leaving on a lengthy journey, you can bless your car. Walk around it clockwise and examine the body, the windows, the wheels and so on.

Visualize a white light all around the car and say the following words:

"Heavenly light, protect my car from all danger, protect my energies so that no harm come to me and that I have a safe and sound journey."

AN EMPLOYMENT CHARMLET

REQUIREMENTS:

GREEN HANDKERCHIEF/ GREEN CLOTH
CARDAMOM SEEDS
BAY LEAF
ROSEMARY

Take a green handkerchief, or a piece of green cloth roughly that size, and lay it flat with one of the corners facing you. Place upon it three cardamom seeds, a bay leaf and some rosemary (or 1 tsp of dried herb).

These herbs surround you in self-confidence and attract energy. Cardamom sweetens your personality and brings out your natural eloquence. Bay leaves are symbols of success and triumph. Rosemary is a herb of achievement and mental alertness. Tie the corners together with a length of string, so that you have a little bundle of herbs. Before each interview, hold this bundle and visualize yourself walking into the interview room, radiating confidence. Imagine yourself being in a position to pick and choose jobs at will. Carry this to your job interviews. And accept that any rejection is a sign from the universe that the job was not right for you.

RELAX ON YOUR HOLIDAY

REQUIREMENTS:

WATER

FLOATING CANDLE

DRIED BASIL

Next time you are out on a holiday with your family, here is a spell that you can perform easily to be at peace with yourself. Fill a bowl with water and a floating candle. Light the candle and gaze into the flame. Gaze for a while into the candle flame and let your mind go blank. Feel your stress pouring into the water and feel your body relax as the stress leaves it.

Sprinkle dried basil over the water, and then chant softly before the candle flame:

"I feel calm, I feel at peace with the universe, so mote it be."

Let the candle burn till the end of it. Pour the water onto the ground and feel your stress and anxiety going with it. Tell yourself that the earth has taken your stress away. Give thanks.

GOOD VIBRATION

REQUIREMENTS:

TWO COLORED CANDLE IN A COMBINATION OF BLACK & WHITE
OR RED & GREEN

PARCHMENT PAPER

Buy a two-colored candle in a combination of
black and white or red and green. The symbolism
of colors repels bad influences and at the same
time attracts good and peaceful vibrations. Write
your intention on a parchment paper and place it
beneath the candle. Light the candle and let it
burn until it is consumed fully or you can light it
for one hour daily, whichever is convenient to you.

As you ignite the candle, repeat this chant:

"Let all the bad vibrations go out.
Let in all the good vibrations,
Let it come in.
Oh! Let my mind be clear,
With harm done to none"

DEVELOP PSYCHIC POWERS

REQUIREMENTS:

WHITE STONE

If you want to develop psychic powers here is a simple stone spell. You need a white stone as white is ruled by the moon, so it is linked with psychic skills. During the night of the full moon, charge your white stone, by giving it the intent to help you develop your hidden psychic powers. You can do this by holding the stone in your hand, and by the power of visualization.

You can repeat this practice on every full moon night to help increase your psychic powers.

PROTECT THOSE WHO WISH TO HARM YOU

REQUIREMENTS:

ONE WHITE CANDLE

CINNAMON INCENSE

BLACK TOURMALINE STONE

When you wish to protect those who wish to harm you, all you need to do is to burn a white candle, some cinnamon incense and a black tourmaline stone.

As you burn the candle and the incense sticks, look at the flames and say the following words:

"I place those who wish to do me harm in God's care and know that all will be well."

Snuff the candle out and thank the universe for protecting you. You can repeat this ritual whenever you feel the need to protect others.

KNOWLEDGE IS POWER

REQUIREMENTS:

- SEA SHELLS
- BEADS
- A SILK POUCH
- SOME FEATHERS
- FEW HAZELNUTS
- VANILLA ESCENCE

If you call upon the spirit of the mighty eagle, it can help you increase your knowledge and power. The hazel was always believed to be a tree of knowledge and hazelnuts - the food of the Gods. The best time to do this spell would be on a Sunday and during the waxing moon.

To start with, you need to decorate the outside of the pouch with beads, shells and feathers. Sprinkle a few drops of vanilla essence on the hazelnuts and put them inside the pouch. Draw up the strings.

Close your eyes and invoke the spirit of the eagle by saying:

"I call you, spirit of eagle, to give me knowledge and courage. Please lend me your power so that I may see ahead clearly."

GIFT OF THE GAB

REQUIREMENTS:

CHARCOAL DISC
YELLOW CANDLE
CITRINE STONE

When you want to increase your communication skills, light a charcoal disc, a yellow candle and keep a citrine stone on your altar to help you synthesize your understanding. Citrine is helpful on an ongoing basis for mental clarity in communicating ideas to others, writing and problem solving. The ritual has to be done during the waxing moon, preferably on a Monday.

As you stare at the flames of the candle, say the following words:

"Power of the moon, bestow fair speech so that I enjoy these gifts to the best of my abilities. I can think and communicate clearly synthesizing information from all levels of my being."

RID BAD HABITS AND FEAR

REQUIREMENTS:

ONE BLACK CANDLE

Light a black candle and as you stare at the flames, say the following words:

"Remove my fear as I cast off all bad habits. Let this not be a sign of weakness for I see it as an initial step to remove any imbalance from my energy field. I would like to let go of any stubborn habit and I trust my abilities to accelerate any new changes and have the courage and determination to work through all fears."

BRIDGE OVER TROUBLED WATERS

REQUIREMENTS:

ONE WHITE CANDLE

When we need to bless ourselves in difficult and troubled circumstances, we can try and follow this spell and see how it works.

Light a white candle and meditate before it by closing your eyes. You can then say the following words:

"Through universal energies, I can experience the abundance of love. I would like you to increase my self-esteem and courage in troubled times and let the light enter my being. Protect me, so that I can be at peace with myself always and trust the messages my feelings are giving me at the moment as I speak up boldly with all that is."

GAIN EMPLOYMENT

REQUIREMENTS:

A PEBBLE (OVAL SHAPED)

ONE YELLOW CANDLE

ONE RED CANDLE

To gain employment, one should carry an amulet or lucky charm when attending interviews. Try to locate an oval shaped pebble and draw an arrow symbol on it pointing upwards towards the sky. You also need one yellow candle and a red candle. As you start your spell, light both the candles on your altar and hold the oval pebble in your palm and visualize yourself having got the job and sitting out to work the next day.

Now, look at the stone and take a deep breath and say:

"Pebble, with the sign of arrow on thee, bring me victory, rich I will be, money, money come hither to me."

Snuff out the candle and carry the pebble with you for interviews. Once you have duly gained employment, throw the pebble into a river or a stream.

FORGET PAST MEMORIES

REQUIREMENTS:

A BLACK CANDLE

TWO THICK STRINGS

MYRRH OIL

Dip the strings in myrrh oil. Tie one end of the string into a knot as this represents memories you want to forget. Tie another knot on the other end as this represents a future free from feelings of the past. Holding one string with the past knot in your left hand allow the past knot cord to burn over the black candle flame totally. Keep the other future knot in a safe place as this might bring you luck.

GUARD AGAINST ENEMIES

REQUIREMENTS:

TWO BLACK CANDLES

QUARTZ CRYSTAL

To guard against your enemies you can burn two black candles on Saturday during the waning moon and also place a quartz crystal between the two candles.

As you burn the candles, chant the following:

"Evil should fail and good should always prevail, evil go hence and may I be protected for ever more."

WORK HARD

When you are feeling discouraged or your mind feels empty, you can try the work hard spell and see whether it really works for you. This spell has to be done during the waxing moon.

REQUIREMENTS:

FIVE AQUAMARINE STONES
A WHITE CANDLE

Set up your place for the spell, burn the white candle and set the aquamarine stones around the candle.
As you light the candle, stare at the flame and say:
"I am reassured and uplifted by the knowledge that my work is my love made visible."
Next, take one aquamarine stone in your hand and say:

"Your energies should give me a sense of continuity that can reassure me when I am discouraged and give my work a sense of value and meaning."

CAST OFF UNWANTED HABITS

If you want to banish unwanted habits, here is a spell that could perhaps help you.

REQUIREMENTS:

THREE ORANGE CANDLES
ONE PEN
RED INK
ONE FIREPROOF DISH
LONG STRIPS OF PAPER.

Write down in that paper the habits you want to do away with. Light the candles during the waning moon and say the following words:

"I would like to dispel my old habits."

As you say this, burn the paper over the flame. Collect the ashes of the burnt paper and throw them into the river or stream.

TO CREATE A SENSE OF BALANCE
IN YOUR LIFE

REQUIREMENTS:

   A YELLOW CANDLE

   A WHITE CANDLE

   A LEPIDOLITE STONE

When you feel that emotional thoughts are restricting your growth, you can try this spell to clear any illusions that you have.

Place the candles on the table and light it. Place the stone in between the white and yellow candle. As you look at the flame and meditate, say the following words:

"I integrate my spiritual awareness by establishing my priorities and acting on them."

TURQUOISE STONE MAGIC

REQUIREMENTS:

TURQUOISE STONE

This stone has magical properties and can be worn, carried or given as a present to a loved one. You can perform a spell with this stone by holding it in your hand on a full moon night and charging it with your intent about what you want from the universe. Then visualize your need about what you need to manifest in your life. Then, look at the full moon and then shift your gaze on the turquoise stone. It can then be worn as it carries good fortune.

SUNDAY SPELLS

REQUIREMENTS:

GOLD JEWELRY OR DRESS IN GOLD OR
SUNFLOWER OR MARIGOLD FLOWER

Sunday is ruled by the sun, so this day can be considered very lucky for personal achievements of any kind. A woman can wear gold jewelry or dress in gold or sunshine yellow and pull some color magic into her life. You could also arrange sunflowers in a vase empowering them as "flowers of the sun" as well as gather up the common marigold flowers and scatter its petals to encourage prosperity, or snack on oranges, enjoying the magical boost it brings to your life.

WHAT'S BREWING

REQUIREMENTS:
    A DECK OF TAROT CARDS
    COURT CARDS OF THE TAROT
    WHITE CANDLE
    CINNAMON INCENSE

This spell is best performed during a full moon on a Saturday night. Place the court cards upside down on the table and light the white candle and incense. Choose four court cards and place them face up on the table. The four cards represent people who would probably come your way and help you in the future.

Pass the cards through the heat of the flame as you say:

"Bring forth help to me and fair counsel."

Show some incense around the cards and say:
"Court cards thou art my wise counselor, look at me with friendly eyes on this full moon day and empower me with all your divine help. Amen."

DETOXIFY

REQUIREMENTS:
DEEP PINK CRYSTALS
DARK ROSE CRYSTALS
HEART-SHAPED CRYSTALS
RUBELITE CRYSTAL
ONE WHITE CANDLE
LAVENDER OIL
FRANKINCENSE OR SANDALWOOD INCENSE

Light the white candle in the space that has to be
cleaned of negative energies. Place the crystals
around the candle, as you burn incense and invoke
the guardian angles to help you in your endeavour.
Smooth or smudge some lavender oil on the
candle and say:
"Together we will release all negative energies that
are not serving us, we shall also donate, recycle
and discard unused items. We shall open our
windows to circulate fresh air and escort all
negativity away."
It's fine to repeat this once a day for any five days
during the waning gibbous moon phase. You will
soon notice huge improvements in all areas of your
life.

SPIRITUAL AWAKENING

REQUIREMENTS:

    TWO WHITE TAPER CANDLES
    PEARL OR MOTHER OF PEARL, QUARTZ CRYSTAL
    LAVENDER OR SAGE INCENSE

Light the white candles on the night of the full moon on a Monday and burn the incense along with it on your altar. Smudge the candle with some lavender oil prior to lighting it. Go out and look at the moon in all her splendor and beauty. In your mind's eye, visualize images of energy; hold the intention of seeing only love and that is what you will see.

Say the following as you look at the flames of the candle:

"O thou unbounded spirit of the universe make me feel thy newness that my mind may be freed from all doubt and fear. Help me to open my spiritual sight so that I can clearly receive heavenly love and guidance for my spiritual work. Amen."

DISPEL DARKNESS - BRING IN LIGHT

REQUIREMENTS:

ONE WHITE CANDLE
ONE BLACK CANDLE
A GOD AND GODDESS CANDLE
LAVENDER OIL
BLACK TOURMALINE CRYSTAL
FRANK INCENSE

During the waning moon on a Saturday, light the candles and smudge lavender oil on the white candle only.

Burn the incense and keep the tourmaline crystals at the side of the candle and say the following:

"Behold the saving light dispelling darkness, Grant, O compassionate one, that I may feel thy abiding presence and dispel all darkness and depression from my heart and fill it with thy radiance that I may shed forth thy light in every act of my life. Amen."

RENDEZVOUS WITH YOUR INNER SELF

REQUIREMENTS:

TWO PINK CANDLES
ONE WHITE CANDLE
JADE AND ROSE QUARTZ CRYSTALS
LAVENDER INCENSE

Light the three candles and the incense on your altar and place the crystals btwteen them. As you look at the flame, ask the universe to sort out your feelings.

Say the following words:
"Help me to forgive others and compassionately see everyone's point of view. Let me approach the situation with a loving heart which allows creative solutions to pour forth. Help me to release feelings of unforgiveness towards others, O guardian Angel! Come into my dreams and act as chimney sweep clearing away any emotional toxins from my heart. Let emotional healings happen for me in a miraculous way. Amen."

GAIN VICTORY

REQUIREMENTS:

SOAP
WATER

Choose an evening of the full moon for your message to reach the universe. It should be early evening, when there is a mild breeze to send your wishes via bubbles, which can be visualized to contain your wishes for gaining victory.
Blow big soap bubbles and mentally picture yourself smiling and happy on your way to victory and then blow these into the universe. Send as many bubbles as you want and be prepared for a pleasant surprise.

GAIN COMFORT SPELL

REQUIREMENTS:
One Vanilla cream candle
Calcite crystal
Sandalwood incense

Everybody loves to have their space and feel comfortable so that they can put their mind at ease. For this spell, one should light a vanilla candle during the waxing moon and hold a calcite crystal in the palm.

Say the following affirmation:

"I work in a cool, gentle, calming manner to ease the reverberations of anxiety and difficulties. I want to be in a peaceful sense of being in control of my experiences so that I can help to bring my feelings into a more relaxed state with minimum of discomfort. I request that I should feel less burdened each time I work with my energies. Amen."

POSITIVE ENERGY SPELL

REQUIREMENTS:
ONE YELLOW CANDLE
ONE ORANGE CANDLE
PATCHOULI, JASMINE SCENTS
ROSE INCENSE

While the moon stimulates yin energy for marriage, it also stimulates yin energy inside the homes. To perform a spell for this, you need to smudge your yellow and orange candles with some scents of either jasmine or patchouli and burn incense on your altar or prayer table. You can perform this spell in the southwest corner of your living room during the waxing moon phase.

As you look at the flame, chant the following words:

"The moon brings lunar energies into my home to invigorate my life with positive thoughts and destroying any negative energies in every corner of your home. Amen."

SPELL TO DEVELOP PATIENCE

REQUIREMENTS:
- AMBER STONE
- ONE WHITE CANDLE
- ONE YELLOW CANDLE

On a Friday, during the waxing phase of the moon, burn a white candle and a yellow candle on your altar. Place the amber between the two candles.

As you look at the burning flame, say:

"I want to be helped to elevate my thoughts to a different level, one of patience and understanding where I can see the meaning in what is taking place without judging the time and effort involved. I ask that I be patient with everybody now and accept myself without judgement. Amen."

CALL UP THE LEOPARD IN YOU

REQUIREMENTS:
   ONE YELLOW CANDLE
   ONE WHITE CANDLE
   CITRINE OR RUBY

When you want to assume leadership, power and position or lovingly guide others, you could try this spell. Light the candles and place the citrine between the candles on your altar, during a waxing moon.

As you gaze at the flames, say out your affirmation to the universe:

"I embrace my powers in a loving way and would like to use it for a greater good. I would like to guide, inspire and motivate others and help me to fearlessly tap into this power."

UNDERSTAND RELATIONSHIP WITH UNIVERSAL ENERGIES

REQUIREMENTS:

OBSIDIAN STONE

Hold the Obsidian stone in your hand and say:

"I would like to understand my purpose with this universe and my relationship with other beings. Let me be a vehicle and enter into other dimensions of reality for a greater understanding of life. My energy should have a releasing effect so that I can understand my true nature and move out of limited thinking to a greater knowledge."

BEAUTY WITHIN

REQUIREMENTS:

CHARCOAL

EARTHEN POT

AGATE CRYSTAL

This spell should be only cast indoors on a new moon day and on any day of the week except Saturday.

As you light a small charcoal in a small earthen pot, take the Agate crystal in your hand and say:

"I would like to be honest and speak honestly with myself and without judgment as it helps me in opening up channels of sharing and giving between myself and others. I want to be sure that what I speak is for the highest good of all mankind and want to be sure that what I say will reach where it is most needed at that moment. Amen."

REMOVE FRUSTRATION

REQUIREMENTS:
   ONE BLACK CANDLE
   BLUE TOPAZ

As you light the black candle on a Saturday during a waning moon phase, hold the blue topaz stone in your hand and say:

"I would like to remove all frustrations from my mind and any doubts that arise thereof when any comparisions are made with my present beliefs and attitudes about myself. I want to remove any negativity and bring in a sense of peace and reassurance and ask the universe for permission and space to assimilate new understandings into my consciousness in a gentle, loving and acceptable way. Amen."

SAFEGUARD AGAINST
UPSETTING EMOTIONS

REQUIREMENTS:

AMETHYST CRYSTAL

If you need a more dramatic way to get rid of
negative emotions, you could try this spell. After
dark in a waning moon phase, hold the amethyst
crystal in your palm and send an affirmation to the
universe.

Say:
"My energy levels should be intensified with all
forms and within Mother Earth herself. I want to
calm my emotional and mental levels so that I can
see clearly what action I may need to take and I
can benefit through the intensity of my experience.
I want to move through any emotional trauma
with more peace. Amen."

FORGET THE PAST

REQUIREMENTS:
- WOOD
- BASIL
- DRIED WEEDS

Firstly, put together a very small bonfire using wood, basil and a bundle of dried weeds.

Stand near the fire and hold the lead crystal in your hand and say:

"I want to get along with my daily life and forget the past. I would not want to be caught in any nostalgic memories or unhappy incidents. Help me to heighten my interest in my daily life, and find each day beautiful. Amen."

GIFTS OF JOY

REQUIREMENTS:

- WHITE CANDLE
- ROSE INCENSE
- RUBY CRYSTAL

During a waxing moon, on a Friday, light the candle and the incense. As you stare at the flame, say:

"I would like to give unconditional love to others and practice expression of will-power through creating positive life force energies for the personal and spiritual growth of all mankind. Amen."

ADD VALUE TO LIFE

REQUIREMENTS:
THREE ORANGE CANDLES,
SUNFLOWERS
ROSE INCENSE
FIRE AGATE CRYSTAL

During the waxing moon, light the orange candles and the rose incense place the agate beside it. Next, as you stare at the flame, say:

"Through my energies, I want to experience joy and add value to my life, give a sense of meaning and purpose regardless of what I have been chosen to do." Snuff the candles and send your intent to the universe. It is fine to repeat this spell for seven days.

INCREASE FORESIGHT

REQUIREMENTS:

AQUAMARINE CRYSTAL

Hold the aquamarine crystal in your palm and send an affirmation into the universe asking, "I hereby ask the powers of this crystal that I might receive enough foresight and self-worth to bring me awareness of the light within me. I would like to act with foresight and in peace with all that is in the universe." Amen.

REMAIN CHEERFUL

REQUIREMENTS:
- ONE ORANGE CANDLE
- ONE YELLOW CANDLE
- ONE CARNELIAN CRYSTAL
- SANDALWOOD INCENSE

On the night of the full moon, light the candles on your altar along with the incense. While placing the crystal beside it, say the following affirmation:

"I would like to share happiness and be cheerful, act more spontaneously and find positive opportunities each day of my life. Amen."

Look at the moon fleeting by amid the clouds and ask for blessings.

ATTAIN EMOTIONAL AWARENESS

REQUIREMENTS:

AMETHYST CRYSTAL

Hold the amethyst crystal in your hand and say:

"I want to attain higher emotional awareness and happiness, as I also want to learn about the power of my emotions. I want to create a positive flow of life force energy and unconditional love in myself and others."

FULL OF FEELINGS

REQUIREMENTS:

ONE WHITE CANDLE
ONE BROWN CANDLE
YELLOW CARNELIAN CRYSTAL

Prepare your altar with your candles and the crystal, light them and say:

"I want my energies to be sensitive to my environment and not indifferent and insensitive in my relationships with others."

Snuff the candle and repeat the same affirmation at least for seven days during the waxing moon phase.

WHERE THERE'S A WILL, THERE'S A WAY

REQUIREMENTS:

TIGER'S EYE CRYSTAL

This spell is from a very old tradition in sympathetic magic. It has to be done on a waxing moon to gain power and on a waning moon phase to remove any weakness of will that may have set in. As you start your affirmation, visualize a white light around you and yourself holding a tiger's eye crystal in your hand as you send prayers to the universe:

"I want to be helped to strengthen my will-power. And as I merge with the divine will I find greater peace and fulfillment."

MOTIVATION

REQUIREMENTS:

JASPER STONE

As you hold the jasper stone in your hand, send out the affirmation:

"I want that jasper's fir quickens my awareness of everything related to my senses. I want to creatively express myself and fight off listlessness, despondency and depression. I want that my sense of joy in being alive and being able to motivate others as well be heightened. Amen."

ACCEPT MY CIRCUMSTANCES

REQUIREMENTS:

JET DIVA

Work with this spell on a waning moon to help banish worries and pray to the universe as you hold a jet diva in your hand.

Say:
"I want to remove grief and worries and accept the reality of circumstances and the acceptance of the inevitability of change. This shall set me free. Amen."

IMPROVE YOUR CREATIVITY

When you need to improve on your creative skills, you can call your guardian angels and say:

"Please help me to improve and enhance my creative skills and delegate time and energy towards my creative pursuits. I wish to call upon you for guidance in all my endeavours. Amen."

CONNECT WITH NATURE

REQUIREMENTS:

FALLEN FEATHERS

GREEN CANDLE

To weave this spell, all you need to do is to look for some fallen feathers outdoors as they are energetically charged by the natural world. Place the feathers in your altar.

As you light a green candle, send your affirmation to the universe:

"Earth Mother! Nurture and protect me, bring in stability and cohesion into my life and the power to manifest whatever I set out to do. Help me connect with nature in all forms to create prosperity and abundance. Amen."

BLAST THROUGH OPPOSITION

Requirements:
Earthen pot
Basil leaves
Herbs
Sesame seeds
Black candle
Sesame oil

When you are attempting to surmount challenges before you, here is a traditional spell you could try. This spell has to be done during the waning moon phase. Place a smoldering earthen pot in the middle of your table, containing some basil leaves, herbs and sesame seeds. Burn a black candle and anoint it with sesame oil.

As you look at the flames, say the following:

"The challenges that I have faced have made me stronger and instead of becoming bitter I want to open my heart with compassion towards others. I would like to overcome any future challenges that come my way. Amen."

Snuff the candle and place the earthen pot outside for the fire to extinguish. It is fine to do this spell at least three times during the waning phase.

SPELL TO PRIORITIZE

REQUIREMENTS:

ONE ORANGE CANDLE

ONE GOLD CANDLE

Cast this spell during the day on a waxing moon and on a Sunday, the day of the Sun God. You need to light one orange and one gold candle.

Light the candles and say: "I want to focus on the areas where my joyful energy can increase. I want to take charge of all my duties and spend time on activities that require attention. I want to be helped so that I can honor my priorities and support my life's endeavors. Amen."

SPREAD YOUR WINGS

Work on this spell at dawn on a waxing moon phase and on any day except Saturday.
As you bow respectively to the eastern direction, facing the rising sun, say:

"I am ready to fly high and welcome new opportunities as well as follow my heart and dreams by spreading my wings."

It is fine to do this spell as many times during the waxing moon.

IMPROVE YOUR TEACHING AND LEARNING SKILLS

REQUIREMENTS:

ONE YELLOW CANDLE

COASTER

Cast the spell on a waxing moon to enhance communication teaching and learning skills.

Light a yellow candle and allow the wax from this candle to drip into a coaster to form a round tablet of about an inch. While the wax is still soft, draw the picture of a teacher and a student. Allow it to cool, then remove intact from the coaster and place it near the candle.

Say the following: "I want to be open to sharing new ideas and knowledge and learning about topics that are not in my sphere of interest. I want to have faith in my teaching and my learning abilities as my mind should be one with the divine."

It is fine to do this spell as many times during the waxing phase but it is important to do the same indoors.

CHECK THIS OUT

REQUIREMENTS:

WHITE CANDLE

You could perform this spell on a waxing moon to draw its strength. As you light a white candle, say:

"I would like to let go of my worries as I am surrounded by my guardian angels. I want to repel all negative energies and focus on light and love instead of fear. My mind should feel free from fear at all times and the divine energies should clear my home, office, vehicle or community of toxic energies. Amen."

TO BE WISE

REQUIREMENTS:

ONE YELLOW CANDLE

ONE GOLD CANDLE

You can cast this spell on a waxing moon phase by lighting a yellow and gold candle and say:

"I hope to be far wiser in the future than I am today and that my inner wisdom should give me all the answers that I seek. I want to put all my ideas into action and make wise decisions in the future. Amen."

STOP AN ARGUMENT

REQUIREMENTS:
- CHARCOAL
- EARTHE POT
- FRANKINCENSE
- BLUE CANDLE
- BLACK CANDLE
- ROOTS, LEAVES & CLOVES

Prepare this spell on a dark or waning moon on Tuesday, a day of fiercely protective Mars for your protection. Light some charcoal in a small earthen pot and burn some frankincense, a blue candle and a black candle.

Place the pot in the middle of the table, add some roots, leaves and cloves into the burning fire, and say: "I wish to express my feelings and ask for the support that I need to move through petty arguments and quarrels. Amen."

Next, extinguish the fire and visualize reconciliation after the quarrel.

CLEAN CLUTTER

REQUIREMENTS:

WHITE CANDLE

This spell should be cast indoors during the waning phase of the moon. Light a white candle and say:

"I want to get rid of all clutter in and around my home and want only positive energies should enter my space."

Let the candle burn till the end, then take the leftover wax and scatter it outside your home in all four directions.

I NEED ANSWERS

REQUIREMENTS:

PINK CANDLE

ROSE QUARTZ CRYSTAL

Light a pale shade of a pink candle during the waxing moon. Wear or hold a rose quartz crystal and your heart will open further to answers you should get from the universe.

As you stare at the flame, say:

"I need answers and I would like to follow my intuitions and work to realize my highest dreams and opportunities. I ask that I get all answers with divine help and know that it is normal and in the light for miracles to occur."

STONES THAT ROCK

REQUIREMENTS:

VELVET POUCH

60 ARTIFICIAL & NATURAL STONE

You can fill a velvet pouch of various artificial and natural stones, about 60 in all. Think of your question and pick the stones at random from the bag. Then count the stones that you have chosen. The odd numbers suggest that a favorable outcome and even numbers indicate a reversal in fortunes.

GREEN-EYED MONSTER

REQUIREMENTS:

WHITE CANDLE

LAVENDER OIL

Cast this spell on any day of the week but on a moonrise. Smear a white candle with lavender oil, avoiding the wick, beginning at the bottom with upward strokes, then from the top to bottom, stopping half way. Repeat this process three times.

Kneeling beside your altar and looking at the flame, say the following:

"I request that all envy and spite in any form should go away, and as I kneel before the candle may I ever be protected from all foes. Amen."

STOP NIGHTMARES

REQUIREMENTS:
10 CARDAMON PODS
1 TSP SALT
15 CLOVES
SOME PEPPERMINT
SOME ROSEMARY SEEDS
ONE WHITE CANDLE
ONE PINK CANDLE

Prepare the following and keep it below your bed to encourage a restful sleep and stop unwanted nightmares.

Light a white and pink candle; place them on your alter. Crush the cloves, cardamon, pepperment and salt to a fine powder. Blend with the herbs and place it in a pouch. As you make the pouch concentrate on peaceful memories and beautiful thoughts.

When you hang the pouch by your bed side, say out loud: "I do not wish to have any frightful nightmares and I want my mind, body and soul to be in perfect balance. Amen."

GEAR UP

Opening your inner gates and trying to find peace within yourself is important to understand where your life is going. For this, you have to perform this ritual alone early in the morning by standing on your feet and making an open gesture to each of the four elemental energies of earth, fire, water and air.

Looking at the eastern direction, say:

"Help me to review my life, where I have been, what I have learned, what patterns I should follow and release into the universe and what I should be grateful for in this life. I would like to grow and learn from this review and try to change and heal anything that is unbalanced. Amen."

CHANGE MY MINDSET

REQUIREMENTS:

RED CANDLE

RED PEN

QUARTZ CRYSTAL

Light a red candle, face south and sit down. Take a piece of paper and with a red pen write down what you would like to change about your thinking process. Carefully fold the paper and burn one end of the paper slightly over the red candle flame. Next, take a quartz crystal and place it on top of the paper.

As you look at the flame, visualize your change in thoughts and say:

"I should speak only goodness, think only kind, look into my own faults and be generous towards and one and all."

LOOKING INWARDS

All of us need to nurture the child within ourselves and we can do this by paying attention to images, feelings and other perceptions along our way. You can write down what you have experienced, and when you have finished, sit down in a chair, take a few breaths and focus on what you have written.

Say the following:

"O God! Help me to nurture the inner child within, what I need to learn and for this help me play, laugh and to be silly and carefree as a child would be, as these activities are important for me right now. Amen."

CONNECT WITH OUTDOORS

You can connect with nature by looking at the
moon on a full moon night and saying:

"I would like to get some fresh air and lunar
energies, Moon Goddess! Help me synchronize my
rhythms to the universal heartbeat. Amen."

DEVELOP GENTLENESS SPELL

REQUIREMENTS:

- ONE BLUE CANDLE
- A WHITE CANDLE
- A MUSICAL INSTRUMENT
- TURQUOISE CRYSTAL

Work on an early waxing moon as you light the candles on your altar and place the turquoise crystal beside it. You can also play a musical instrument of your choice to bring in the natural harmony and rhythm. Next, hold the turquoise in your hand and meditate upon this blue color.

Say:
"I want to bring in the qualities of gentleness and tranquility and surround myself with gentle people, situations and environment. Amen."

MANNERISM MAKEOVER

REQUIREMENTS:

ORANGE CANDLE

Draw a circle and honor the four elements of air, fire, water and earth. Light an orange candle saying:

"Cleanse my mind, Spirit pure; fill my thoughts with good mannerisms. I seek this flame and honor your presence and ask you to hear my prayer."

It is fine to repeat this spell as many times in the waxing phase of the moon.

PLAY ON

REQUIREMENTS:

> WHITE CANDLE
>
> EMERALD GREEN CRYSTAL

For a healthy lifestyle, light a white candle in a waxing moon phase and hold an emerald green crystal in the palm of your hand.

Say:
"I would like to eat a healthful diet, get adequate rest and exercise freely so that my health situation is healed."

TOP OF THE WORLD

REQUIREMENTS:

RED CANDLE

If you want to feel at the top of the world, you can help yourself grow stronger as each day goes by. This spell can be performed on all the waxing phases of the moon especially on Fridays. Light a red candle and ask the universe to grant you all the protection and guidance, so that you are not fooled by illusions of fear and worry.

You can look up at the moon passing by and say:

"I would like to shore up confidence within myself and develop self-esteem."

It is fine to repeat this practice as many times during the waxing moon.

HANGOVER SPELL

REQUIREMENTS:
SEA SALT

BLACK CANDLE

Before you start performing this spell, take some sea salt and sprinkle a little on the sectors of your home as it carries the powerful cleansing energies of the ocean. Light a black candle in any of your rooms and visualize that you have totally abstained from drinking alcohol in any form.

Say the affirmation:
"I really don't want to think about my bad habit and I perceive this not as a problem but as a challenge to get over. I want to be helped to grow out of it rather than be weighted by it. Amen."

GETTING A GOOD NIGHT'S SLEEP

REQUIREMENTS:

YELLOW CANDLE

This is a simple spell that can be done often whenever sleep patterns change. Every night before going to sleep, light a yellow candle and say:

"I want to release any unbalanced energies which I absorbed during the day. I do not want any negative energy to effect my conscious mind, emotions or physical body for I am indeed the light!"

It is fine to repeat this prayer whenever you need a good night's sleep.

HONOR YOUR COMMITMENTS

REQUIREMENTS:

YELLOW CANDLE

Cast this spell on a waxing moon to honor your commitments and on any day of the week apart from Saturday.

Light a yellow candle and as you look at the flame, say:

"Garden angels, look well and kindly upon me as I honor my commitments towards others. I invoke the lady of the moon on this night to give me powers to be true to myself and to others."

Snuff the candle and give thanks. It is fine to repeat this spell as many times during the waxing moon.

SPELL FOR CLOSENESS AND HEALING

REQUIREMENTS:

WHITE CANDLE

This spell is again associated with the mother moon and it can be performed on the night of the full moon.

Light a white candle and as you stare at the flame, say:

"My personal will and the emotions that accompany it are in harmony with my higher will. I would like to feel close to my family and those dear to me as I release all nervous tension and feel calm and relaxed."

SILVER LINING

REQUIREMENTS:
- THREE ORANGE CANDLE
- THREE WIHTE CANDLE
- ROSEMARY SEEDS
- ORANGE POWDER

You know you have the right to feel optimistic in every situation and you can perform a simple spell which will always makes you feel hopeful. In the waxing phase of the moon, light three white and three orange candles. Keep them alternatively and light them one after the other from right to left.

Sprinkle some rosemary seeds, some orange powder over the flames and say:

"My optimistic outlook should keep me cheerful and pleasant as each day goes by."

You can repeat this spell whenever you want to feel upbeat.

MIRROR, MIRROR TELL ME THE TRUTH

REQUIREMENTS:

WHITE CANDLE

PAPER

BLACK MARKER PEN

When you want to know the truth and feel quite in the dark about someone or something, you could try this spell and see if it works. On a waning moon, light a white candle on your altar and draw 20 wands on a piece of paper, some upright and some reversed.

Next, with a black marker pen in your hand, close your eyes, go over the paper and think of the person who has lied to you and try to circle one of the wands drawn on the paper.

If the wand is reversed, it means that the person had been deceitful and misused his or her powers and calls for excessive caution. If you circle an upright wand, it indicates honesty, righteousness and a favorable outcome of events and shows the person did not have any selfish motives.

TO WISH UPON A STAR

REQUIREMENTS:

WHITE CANDLE

PURPLE CANDLE

For this spell, on a clear moonlit night, when the moon is waxing, you could perform this spell to increase abundance. You can wish upon a star and state your wishes aloud.

The spell could be done preferable on a Sunday.

Light a white candle and a purple one, and using the violet flame meditation, say:

"I wish upon this star for purpose, guidance and optimism and the present completion of one step gives me a sense of continuity in my life. Amen."

FLOWER POWER

REQUIREMENTS:

FRESH DAISIES

You could try this spell to know whether your lover loves you or not. This is an easy and valuable spell as it gives you insights about your relationship, friendship, decisions and brings in the balance between the male and female energies. Pluck some fresh daisies from your garden or buy them from a florist.

As you pluck the petals, keep saying:

"He or she loves me or loves me not"

Keep doing this till you reach the last petal. The answer to your question lies in the last petal that you pluck.

AVOID SETBACKS

REQUIREMENTS:

BLUE CANDLE

If you need to avoid minor setbacks in your life, you could work on this spell. On a waning moon phase, light a blue candle on your altar and say:

"I call upon my guardian angel and ask that I avoid all setbacks in my life, as I would like to appreciate myself and see how beautiful I am right now."

Spend some time alone with yourself to find answers to what is really happening in your life, and try to avoid harsh situations and people. It is fine to repeat this spell as many times during the waning moon and your luck should change for the better within one moon cycle.

INSPIRE AND INFLUENCE OTHERS

REQUIREMENTS:

WHITE CANDLE

When you need to inspire people, you could try this spell. On a waxing moon phase, on a Thursday sacred to Jupiter, light a white candle and say:

"I would like to succeed and inspire others in their endeavors. I would like to emanate the awesome qualities of love, strength and unwavering faith in all that I do."

BRACELET SPELL

REQUIREMENTS:

SILVER BRACELET MADE OF CERTAIN EMPOWERED CRYSTALS LIKE JADE, PEARLS & EMERALDS

You can wear a bracelet made of certain empowered crystals like emeralds, pearls and jade, mounted in silver. On a night of the full moon take your bracelet and catch the reflection of the moon and in this way you could empower your jewellery. This way you will soon understand these stones and the power that lies with it.

TO HEAVEN AND BACK

REQUIREMENTS:

TWO WHITE CANDLE

This spell could be done at any phase of the moon by trying to connect with your loved ones in heaven. Burn two white candles and try to calm your mind as you sit to meditate.

As you meditate, you can perhaps feel their presence in these quieter moments. These truly are visitations and you can trust your intuitions. You could also have them visiting you in your dreams on that particular night. This will help you understand that your loved ones are safe in heaven and want the same for you.

GIVE AND RECEIVE

REQUIREMENTS:

AMETHYST CRYSTAL

You can cast this spell during the waxing moon phases and send your affirmations to the universe for unconditional love. Hold an amethyst crystal in your hand, look to the east and say:

"I want to be willingly receptive and let go of my old patterns of thinking about myself and others. Instead, I want a sense of emotional security that allows me to be open to all new experiences. I want to be reassured that I will not fail in my new endeavors of giving and receiving from and towards others. Amen."

WIN-WIN SITUATION

REQUIREMENTS:

THREE PALE BLUE CANDLE

WINE

This is best cast on a waxing moon for a win-win situation and for solutions that are fair to everyone involved. Light three pale blue candles on your altar and drink a cup of wine in the evening before you do your spell. Keep another cup of wine on your altar besides the candle to represent the other person or party concerned. As you look at the burning candle flame, say positive affirmations to keep your spirits high. Visualize your conversations with words about the situation that are only positive and optimistic.

CRYSTAL CLEAR INTENTION

REQUIREMENTS:

SUGALITE OR SUGALITE PENDANT
ONE BLUE CANDLE
ONE PURPLE CANDLE

If you want to be clear about what you desire and focus upon your goal, you can do this spell once a week early in the morning. Light the candles and place the sugalite pendant by its side. Ask the universe to channel profound messages to help you to be clear with your intentions for the week. Snuff out the candle and give thanks.

TO BE A ROLE MODEL

REQUIREMENTS:

A PICTURE OF A LION OR YOUR ROLE MODEL TO BE KEPT
ON YOU ALTAR
ONE WHITE CANDLE
ONE RED CANDLE

Work this spell any time of the day. Light your candles and keep the pictures on the altar and say:

"I want to be courageous and stand up for what I believe in. I want to reflect the qualities of a lion including bravery, courage, focus and elegant movements."

Next, look at the picture of the Lion God on the table and call upon it to boost your confidence and courage.

CLEAR CONFUSION

REQUIREMENTS:

ONE WHITE CANDLE

Cast this spell on a waxing moon and on any day of the week. As you light a white candle, to clear your doubts and confusion, say:

"I would like to move forward in my path without confusion and hindrances. Amen."

THESE COULD BE THE ANSWERS

REQUIREMENTS:

OIL BURNER

TEA LIGHT CANDLE

CHURCH CANDLE (WHITE)

You need to know that you should pay attention to the thoughts and ideas that come to your mind because these could well be the answers. Burn one oil burner along with a tea light candle and some camphor just to remove any negativity from the room where you are meditating. To help you focus and concentrate on your thoughts and ideas light a church candle, preferably white in colour.

As you face the east, say:

"I want my answers to come to me in the form of repetitive thoughts and ideas, I want to be tapped into the Divine wisdom now so that I can take notice and record my thoughts. I trust that this information which comes to me shall help me in my life's journey."

IMPROVE YOUR SITUATION

REQUIREMENTS:

WHITE CANDLE

Work on a waning moon phase for casting this spell and turning anxiety away. Light a white candle and say:

"I want to be helped to fine tune my daily situation and I want to avoid doing anything impulsively which can be unnecessarily risky. I want to have a sense of reassurance and Divine help that my decisions are in harmony with the long-term goals that I have set for myself."

FORGIVE OTHERS

REQUIREMENTS:

WHITE CANDLE

INCENSE

When you want to let go of resentment, judgement and anger, here is one simple spell that you can try. Play some soft music, light a white candle and some incense of your choice, take some deep breaths and do a short visualization or meditation.

As you visualize, you can say aloud:
"I would like to release the toxins of negative energies and forgive the person or situation so that I can move on with my dreams."

TO BEGIN THE PROCESS OF CHANGE

REQUIREMENTS:

SILVER ORNAMENT

When you feel you are stuck in a rut and want to get ahead in life, here is a spell that can be easily performed at home. If you have a silver ornament like a pendant with you, it can be programmed to release constrictions that keep you away from the process of change happening in your life. Hold the silver ornament in your palm and send an affirmation to the universe saying:

"I want to increase my sensitivity to my emotional nature and want that my energies be gentle, harmonizing and flowing and bring with it the desired changes I need in this lifetime."

AWAKEN YOUR ENERGIES

REQUIREMENTS:

RED CANDLE

We find that in times of stress we often forget to breathe. So, here is a simple spell to help you awaken your energies. During the waxing moon, you can light a red candle and say:

"I would like to invigorate myself with deep and steady breaths and inhale fresh air thereby energize my body, mind and spirit. Amen."

It is fine to do this as many times as you want to during stressful times.

MAKE A STEADY PROGRESS

REQUIREMENTS:

RED PEN

When you need to make steady progress in life, you should understand that it's not perfection but progress that really matters. Write down on paper with a red pen your ideas and thoughts on how you want to recognize this progress. Light a candle in a waxing moon phase and carefully fold the paper into a rectangular shape - try to burn part of the corners over the flame. Then, keep the paper near the candle and try to visualize yourself helping people along your way, and forgiving yourself for what you've done or not done.

ARTFUL VISIONS

REQUIREMENTS:
YELLOW CANDLE

If you want to attend formal classes, work with a mentor or develop your creativity, try this spell. This should be done on a waxing moon to enhance your creative and artistic skills.

As you light a yellow candle, say:
"I want to use my days wisely by pursuing higher education, newfound ideas, and better self-esteem. Help me in my task so that I walk through it with full faith."

LOOK DEEPER

REQUIREMENTS:

BIG BOWL OF WATER

WHITE CANDLE

INCENSE

When you need to look deeper beyond the surface of any situation and find answers, here is a simple spell you can perform. You need a big bowl of water to look into and see your reflection, a white candle and some incense of your choice.

As you light the candle look deeply into the water and ask:

"I am not currently unaware of important information and I wish to be able to look deeper for a better understanding"

Next, sit still for 10 minutes and listen to your inner truth.

BELIEVE IT OR NOT

REQUIREMENTS:
CHARCOAL
EARTHEN POT
SESAME SEED
CINNAMON OIL
STONE (RECTANGULAR)
OIL PAINT
PAINTBRUSH

At times, it is important for us to believe in ourselves and in others. You could carry out this spell during any moon phase, except the dark moon. Light some charcoal in an earthen pot and sprinkle some sesame seeds and two drops of cinnamon oil. Get a stone, preferably rectangular in shape, one fine artist paintbrush and some oil paint. Next, paint onto the stone a symbol of a woman with her hands opening upwards symbolizing universal faith and belief.

Pass this stone through the incense smoke and through the candle flame and say:

"I would like to appreciate the essential goodness in others and believe in them as well as remove any doubt about my own capabilities as an individual."

It is fine to repeat this whenever you are feeling low and need to believe in yourself.

BUBBLE SPELL

In case you are feeling troubled all the time and need to have peace of mind and get away for sometime, you could try this visualization spell. Try to imagine that you are inside a huge bubble with white light to protect you for peace and you are flying in the sky against unruly winds. As you float by, you will feel a sense of tranquility and calm and gain inner peace. It is fine to break out of your bubble and practice the same at troubled times.

PENDANT SPELL

REQUIREMENTS:

PENDANT WITH STONE LIKE JASPER, JADE, ONYX RUBY

You can easily get a pendant with certain stones engraved on it like jasper, jade, onyx and ruby. Energize the pendant by keeping it out on a full moon night and wear it the next day. Send positive affirmations about what you desire to achieve and don't be surprised if you find your wishes coming true.

ALL EYES ON ME

When you need to be in the limelight and want to draw attention to yourself at a party, all you need to do is this simple spell. Just a few hours before you attend this party, say an affirmation:

"I want to express the joy of being alive and only people of high integrity come to me and appreciate me, so that I too can understand how beautiful the world is."

TO BE AN ACTIVIST

When you have been asked to champion a cause or a social issue, here is a simple spell that can boost your interest and confidence level. During the waxing moon phase, say the following:

"I want to increase my passion for such kind of work and make a commitment to serve in some capacity to heal those situations and to the best of my ability."

BIBLIOGRAPHY

1. Fernie,Williams T.;
The Occult and Curative Powers of Precious Stones; Edition 1973; Rudolf Steiner Publications.

2. Santopietro Nancy;
Fengshui and Health; Edition 2002; B. Jain Publishers.

3. www.worldoffengshui.com

4. www.wester-mysteries.org